New Thinking • New Strategies • New Expectations

New Realities at the Crossroads of Business and Race

Melvin J. Gravely II, Ph.D.

Edited by Barbara McNichol
Cover design and inside layout by Ad Graphics, Inc.
Internal graphics designed by Amy Winegardner
Printed in the United States of America.

Gravely II, Melvin J.,
What Is the Color of Opportunity?
New Realities at the Crossroads of Business and Race

ISBN 978-0-9656194-0-0

Library of Congress Control Number: 2010937069

Mailing address:
Impact Group Publishers
P.O. Box 621170, Cincinnati, OH 45262-1170

ACKNOWLEDGMENTS

I am a blessed man. I have great relationships with committed, generous, and supportive people.

To my wife, Chandra, who is always at the front of the line to support me. Her quiet confidence lifts me when I'm struggling and sometimes doubting. Chandra, your support is unwavering and a mere thank you is just not enough. I love you.

To my sons, James and Martin, I thank you for your patience. Writing books takes a lot of time and hours of focus. You guys gave me the space to get it done.

To my daughter, Cheree, who is now a grown woman with opinions and insights of her own, I thank you for your constant words of encouragement.

So many people touched this book to help me make it my best ever. These words are my attempt at expressing my sincere appreciation. Your support is invaluable. Thank you all: Angie Avery, Vanessa Freytag, Sylvester Hester, Arlene Koth, D. Mitchell, Lisa Switalski, Sandra Talley, Scott Vowels, Otis Williams, and Stan Williams.

A special thank you to Crystal German and Joan Fox. Crystal, you became my thinking partner on the content of this book. Simply no one knows this subject matter better than you do. I thank you for pushing (and pushing and pushing) me so hard to get it right. Joan, your creativity and command of words released the story and let it flow. Thank you for always being willing to review my work "just one more time."

Special gratitude to Robin Bischoff for all of the things you do every day. Thank you.

To Messer Construction. Your organization is an example of both commitment and innovation  in the development of sustainable minority businesses. Thank you for your early and ongoing support of my work and for your leadership in the construction industry. Your investments in diversifying your base of suppliers have made a difference.

4

TABLE OF CONTENTS

Not having a problem
to fix doesn't mean
we're doing well.

CHAPTER
1

WE HAVE
A PROBLEM

Fenton Rice had a million thoughts going through his head. He had lost his vice president of operations to a competitor and he needed to focus on what his company would do to replace her. The company had just won another contract with Republic, its largest customer by far. The contract was much smaller than they had hoped, but Fenton had learned to take what he could get. Business could be better, but it wasn't his first time facing challenges. That was how he lived. Things were always changing with his business. It was like he moved from struggle to struggle with an occasional new contract in between. But at least they continued to be awarded more work. *That's how it is as a minority business. Nothing is given to you and every challenge weighs on you*, he concluded. Although he'd been challenged often in his 14 years in business, Fenton was successful by many measures—an African American business owner with a solid track record and quality customers. His business had grown over the years. He had often been recognized with awards as a successful minority business owner. Other minority owners wished they stood in his shoes. But *he* knew how tenuous his company's situation was.

Fenton was sitting in his office with the door closed so he could finish a few things before he went to his Roundtable meeting. The Roundtable was a small group of minority entrepreneurs. One of the members had given the group a short article to read, and Fenton didn't want to show up without having read it. *They may decide to discuss it during the meeting*, he thought. He pulled the piece of paper from a stack on his desk and began to read. It was from *Minority Business Owner Magazine*.

Don't Miss the Signs: How a Changing Environment Can Kill Your Business

Let me tell you a little story about how the changes in minority business development can force you to rethink your business. Years ago, I owned a company with a few other partners. It was back in the *Set Aside Era*, the first of the three eras of minority business development. That was back when they set projects aside and only minority firms could pursue them. There's still a little of that going on today but not much. We started the business because there were few minorities in the field. Our minority status was our competitive advantage.

Set Aside Era
— Projects set aside for minority firms
— Few minority firms to compete
— "Legislated" inclusion

That may sound crazy in today's terms but it was so crazy it worked. We grew quickly. We made money. We were a part of interesting projects. We didn't get a chance to do the interesting parts of the interesting projects but at least we were "on the team." Then things began to change. We couldn't get anyone to give us an opportunity to do the next, more significant tier of work. It became more and more difficult for us to get contracts. The contracts we did get were smaller and less lucrative. What used to be the uninteresting parts of projects became the mundane parts. We struggled to keep good talent because talented people didn't want to work on mundane things.

The situation wasn't good. So what had changed from when we started the business? At the time, we couldn't figure it out. What we discovered later was the era had changed from the *Set Aside Era* to the *Access Era*, the second era of minority business development. The new era changed the rules. The *Access Era*

was designed to get minority firms information about opportunities, access to meet decision makers, and access to the technical assistance everyone thought we needed. But the Access Era provided no guaranteed access to *contracts*. So we got caught in the Access Era with a competitive advantage that only worked in the Set Aside Era.

Access Era
— Access to information
— Access to technical support/education
— Access to decision makers
— "Desired" inclusion

From then on, we struggled as a business. I remember the night it hit me how out of step we had become. In our monthly managers meeting, I asked if anyone could step us through the process of getting work not set aside for minority firms. How do businesses work the system to *see* an opportunity? Then how do they *seek* that opportunity? And finally, how do they *secure* it? None of us could articulate the process.

We missed the warning signs. The changes in the approach to minority business were subtle, but there were clear warning signs along the way. Worse yet, we lied to ourselves about our true competitive position.

Although the article didn't state who the author was, Fenton totally related to the story. He read on.

We are at the tail end of the *Access Era* now and moving quickly into what I'm calling the . . .

Fenton's office phone rang and startled him. He set down the article and reached for the phone.

"Fenton Rice," he answered.

"Fenton, Ralph Blaine from Jaeton City Bank," the voice said.

"Hey, Ralph. Do you have any news on the renewal of our line of credit?"

"Yes I do, and we need you to come in to talk with us about it."

"Oh. Okay. We've not had to do that in the past. Is there something wrong?" Fenton probed.

"There are just some issues we want to talk through," Ralph confirmed. "Are you available next Tuesday at ten a.m.?"

"Let me see," Fenton said pulling up his calendar on the computer. "Yes, I can make that work."

"Thanks. We'll see you then," and they said their goodbyes.

"This can't be good," Fenton said aloud. "They never ask you to come in to give *good* news."

Fenton picked up the phone and dialed Michelle's office extension. Michelle had been with Fenton from the start. She was his most trusted executive, and she had been through the company's challenges and successes right along with him.

"This is Michelle," she answered.

"Hey, Michelle, it's Fenton. I just got a call from Ralph Blaine at the bank."

"What did he say?" she asked.

"He asked me to come to their office to talk about the renewal of our line of credit."

"Well, they didn't say no . . . at least not yet," Michelle said. "What do you think they saw they didn't like?"

"I'm not sure, but you know we've had a rough go of it the past few months."

"I doubt they're holding up the renewal on our line of credit because of the last few months. Our company hasn't been in a good space for a few years. We seem to think that *not* having a problem to fix means we're doing well. And that's not necessarily true."

Fenton thought about her point. "You're right about that. That's exactly what's happened to us," he said with a tone of reluctance. Then he revived his energy. "Michelle, I'll need your help to prepare for the meeting with Ralph."

"I'll start working on it now," Michelle replied, eager to dive in.

"Great. I've got to get going to my Roundtable meeting. Talk with you when I get back."

Completely distracted now, Fenton couldn't stop wondering what was going on at the bank. He shook his head as he stuck the article about three eras into his ever-present leather portfolio. He'd have to finish reading it later. *Cute story but that guy just wasn't paying attention to his business,* he thought. *I don't care what 'era' you're in, you need contracts and capital to survive.* He grabbed his car keys and hurried from his office so he wouldn't be late for the Roundtable meeting.

CHAPTER 2

THINGS HAVE
<u>CHANGED</u>

J immy Edwards was talking in a low voice as Fenton walked into his Roundtable meeting. It was easy to tell this conversation was difficult for Jimmy. "It's all coming apart. We may not make it through the quarter and surely not to the end of the year. Our contract with PPC Global ended last year and we've been unable to win another significant opportunity. We've run out of financial resources and no one seems willing or able to help us."

Everyone just listened.

"And I get the sense it's not just us. I think the whole idea of minority business development is falling apart," Jimmy continued. "Major organizations have already diluted their programs by adding everyone and his brother as a certified class."

"I keep hearing their spending numbers are going up and they're reaching their goals. But is anyone here seeing similar

ROUNDTABLE MEMBERS

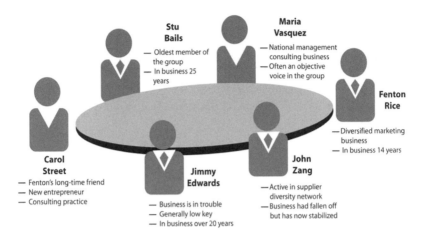

Stu Bails
— Oldest member of the group
— In business 25 years

Maria Vasquez
— National management consulting business
— Often an objective voice in the group

Fenton Rice
— Diversified marketing business
— In business 14 years

Carol Street
— Fenton's long-time friend
— New entrepreneur
— Consulting practice

Jimmy Edwards
— Business is in trouble
— Generally low key
— In business over 20 years

John Zang
— Active in supplier diversity network
— Business had fallen off but has now stabilized

effects in your business?" asked Stu Bails, the oldest member of the group. His packaging business had been around for over 25 years. Seated across from Stu, John Zang had once been the poster child for supplier diversity. His firm had shrunk over the last five years but appeared to have stabilized. Maria Vasquez, owner of a national management consulting business, often offered a calming voice to the group. Carol Street, a long-time friend of Fenton's, had been his banker years ago and then became his main contact when she worked at Republic. Carol knew the inside story about how major buyers regarded minority businesses—and how their motivations had changed over time. She now owned a relatively new consulting practice. Fenton thought of himself as a junior member of the group because of his young age compared with the others. He'd come from obscurity and built a sizable business. Although he'd developed fewer "big hitter" relationships than the others, his company's performance over the years had gained him their respect.

The group members knew each other well. They'd been meeting twice a month for more than three years with a single-minded mission: helping each other grow their businesses. In doing so, they shared information about opportunities, exchanged contacts, and referred resources. In addition, they brought concerns to the group to get input. Fenton felt a level of trust among the members but always wondered if they were truly authentic with each other. After all, they kept saying how well they were doing—*too* well for him to believe they were also being honest. *If things were so good, why were they always complaining about the lack of opportunity?* Fenton questioned. Jimmy's announcement about being in trouble just may have proved his point.

Maria looked around the table and asked somberly, "Well, how are the rest of us doing?"

Silence. Each member seemed to be waiting on the other to speak first.

Fenton spoke up. "Well, we've been seeing an upturn in the interest from some major organizations, but it's becoming more difficult to convert their interest into actual contracts."

John agreed. "There's a lot of talk about it, but Fenton is right. There's little action behind their stated interest. And when they show any kind of interest, it costs us money to pursue their contracts, especially if we don't have a realistic chance to win them."

Stu chimed in. "It seems like it's becoming more important for these organizations to *appear* to want to do business with minority firms than for them to *actually* do business with us."

"Hold on. Do you guys really believe that?" Fenton asked. "I mean all of our businesses are where they are because of the contracts we either have now or *have* had with these same organizations we're talking about."

"I just think the game has changed," stated Stu flatly. "They all have minority firms they work with regularly, and they have them at the level where they feel comfortable. And don't get me started with some of these so-called joint ventures. They're simply a new way to create a good old-fashioned front company. But the truth is, more and more minority firms are entering the market, while the volume of minority opportunities isn't growing."

"Minority opportunities?" asked Fenton.

"You know what I mean. These organizations all have their spending goals," Stu clarified.

"The term has become 'diverse firms.' It's not just 'minority firms' anymore," John added.

Fenton leaned back in his chair and looked up at the ceiling as the others kept talking. *This all just sounds old and tired,* Fenton thought. *Minority opportunity? Is Stu right about this? Is this how decision-makers in major organizations think? Is there only a* limited *amount of opportunity for our businesses? Are appearances more important to them than actually doing business with minority firms?*

"We're missing something, guys," Fenton interjected. "What we're experiencing feels like they just don't care as much as they used to—like there's a cap on our opportunity. There *has* to be more to what's going on than that."

"These major organizations are what we thought they were," John responded.

"They probably are," Fenton said. "But exactly what did we think they were? We're not a bunch of business owners who haven't gotten our shot. Come on, let's be fair here. Let's not start lying to ourselves. We started and grew our businesses in the context of supplier diversity and minority business development. We all used these programs to get whatever we have gained. That doesn't mean we're not talented and our businesses aren't capable. *But* we can't forget the impact their interest in minority business has had."

"I would have started my business and grown it with or without those programs," John protested.

"Okay. Then *why* does their apparently fading interest in minority business bother you?"

"It's about principle, Fenton. They make bold promises and don't come through," Stu grumbled.

"It's not about principle for me," stated John. "It's about opportunity. We can't grow without access to opportunity, and I'm just not seeing it."

Jimmy, who hadn't said much, leaned forward and added, "That's not the worst of it. I hear some of the top CEOs in Jaeton City are meeting soon to talk about *ending* their support of all minority business programs."

"Really? What prompted that?" Carol asked.

"Although they're stating lots of reasons, the main one is they're not seeing much in the way of results. They feel like they keep investing but not much changes and they get blamed anyway," Jimmy explained. "Right now, they say they're taking an *objective* look at the situation to help them come up with an ultimate decision," concluded Jimmy as his fingers formed quotation marks around the word "objective."

"If they start withdrawing their support, there will be no stopping it. The rest of them take their cues from the top business leaders," Carol said.

Everyone in the room knew she was right.

CHAPTER

3

VITAL SIGNS

Fenton left the Roundtable meeting deep in thought. Once he reached his car, he switched the radio's channel to the public station. Diane, the familiar-sounding host of the business show, was interviewing a business owner named Jasper Turpin.

"I spent years drifting in business instead of actually heading some place," Jasper confessed. "The drifting took its toll on us. We were always in and out of trouble. We tried a lot of stuff. Things would get better for a time but we would always find ourselves dealing with our same problems. We had mixed performances with our customers and couldn't convince them to give us a shot at larger opportunities. We were experiencing shrinking profit margins. And it was also difficult to recruit and retain top talent." Jasper Turpin paused. "You know, Diane," he said frankly. "It was weird. It's wasn't like we were failing, but we just weren't succeeding."

This guy's issues sound a lot like mine, Fenton thought. In his business, Fenton could just never get over the hump to feeling confident about his ability to sustain the business. What was happening to Jimmy Edwards from the Roundtable was a viable possibility for his business, too.

"Well," Diane responded. "We're interviewing you today partly because of your story but also because of your business success. What changed in the business that led to your success?"

"This interview isn't long enough for me to talk about everything that's changed," Jasper said laughing. "But all of the changes started when I got better vital signs."

Fenton turned up the volume.

"Vital signs?" Diane asked.

"Yes. We started down a better road when we focused on profit, growth, and wealth, which we see as the vital signs of the business. Together, the three provide a prism through which we could view everything."

Fenton liked the clarity of what he was hearing, but still, this wasn't new to him. Or maybe he was more interested in listening because of his current business pressures and the Roundtable conversation he'd just left. Although he liked the message, he wasn't sure it fit for his business.

"Profit, growth, and wealth. Those sound straightforward. But Jasper, can you briefly explain each of them to our listeners?" Diane asked.

"Diane, we made a point of noticing that strong, thriving companies focus on these three things. Profit reflects our short-term objective. Growth gives us the ability to accumulate profitable opportunities over time. And wealth is the long-term outcome of our focus on profit and growth. And these became our focus. We believe this gives us the right balance of managing our short-term business needs with our long-term aspirations."

"I understand. But this change had to have implications on how you did business. For example, how did this 'prism' affect how you decided which contracts to pursue?" she asked.

"That's the idea," Jasper said chuckling. "We *wanted* it to have implications on our business, and a perfect example is how we selected which contracts to pursue. We used to decide based on our ability to win a contract, which is not bad in itself. But we learned that focusing on our vital signs made us more strategic. So now we first ask, can we make money? Based on what we do well, can we then expand that opportunity with other clients? Will it lead to wealth for our business over time?"

That has to take a lot of discipline, Fenton thought. *Contracts are our lifeblood. We would have to say 'no' to some opportunities. Can we afford to do that? But it's obvious we need a strategy that's more comprehensive than a single-contract opportunity.* Fenton was mulling through the idea of using these vital signs as a new way to view his own business. He turned his attention back to the interview.

"I get it, Jasper, but what do you think is so special about these three?"

"Diane, your question is right on, and I'm glad you asked it because I would hate for your listeners to go away with any misunderstanding. The answer to 'why these three' is because they work for us. They may not work for others. Doctors refer to pulse, blood pressure, and respiration as vital signs. We refer to profit, growth, and wealth as the vital signs of a healthy business. That's why they became our strict focus."

"Have you had any pushback about your focus on wealth? It seems a bit self-serving." Diane inserted this delicate question.

"I know what you're saying," Jasper responded. "The concept of wealth bothers a lot of people and I understand that. We're not pursuing wealth because we're selfish and greedy. Wealth is the by-product of a business's success. It's how we impact our community, invest in our futures, and take care of our people. Wealth is the component of business that provides continuation beyond our lifetimes. Everyone should want a business to be wealthy. Yes, we were always committed to giving back, but we can only give back what we have to give. The more we have, the more we can give."

Although Fenton and his peers talked about wealth creation, he honestly wasn't sure the concept was real in their minds. Admittedly, he was hesitant to profess wealth as his goal—maybe due to his upbringing. *Perhaps I have a deep psychological hang-up about not being worthy of wealth,* he thought. He pulled his car into the parking lot in front of his office building, then picked up an envelope from his passenger seat, turned it over, and began to take notes. *Vital signs—a new prism,* he wrote. *Profit, growth, wealth.*

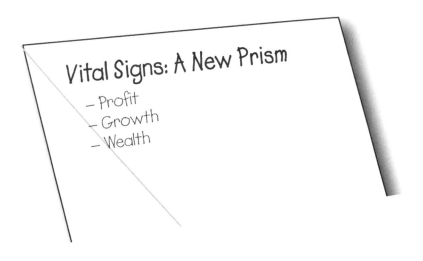

This was all good for Jasper Turpin, thought Fenton considering his notes. "But I'm not sure it's that simple for Fenton Rice," he said aloud.

* * *

With all the concerns of his business, the call from the bank, and the Roundtable conversation, Fenton's brain was spinning. *Too much,* he thought. He needed to get his head clear and he hadn't talked to Hugh, his long-time mentor, in months. Fenton reached for his cell phone. Spending some time with Hugh Belden seemed like a good idea.

Just because we always have, doesn't mean we always should.

CHAPTER 4

THE PERFECT STORM
OR A WAKE-UP CALL?

"**M**y folks tell me I don't understand," said the man at the head of the table, a manila folder in his hand. "And they're right. Based on what I see, I *don't* understand. We have five minority business support organizations in this community. They tell me between our government agencies and various non-profits, our community invests eight hundred thousand dollars a year to care for and feed those programs. Many of us also have supplier diversity programs inside our organizations. And I still have the leader of the black ministers and the head of the Hispanic coalition telling me the lack of success for minority businesses is my fault."

Wade Blair, the energetic new CEO of Republic, paused to catch his breath and reload his thoughts. Although Wade was new to Jaeton City, the size of Republic Corporation and its influence in the community has made Wade one of its most influential leaders in a short time. In his early 40s but appearing even younger, Wade liked to communicate in an animated manner.

CEO MEETING ATTENDEES

Mary Michael
— Leader of the group
— Open but not well versed in minority business

Wade Blair
— New CEO of Republic
— Young and results oriented
— Open minded and willing to listen

Don Dressel
— Has knowledge of minority business
— Moderately supportive but not significantly

Bob Smithton
— Has knowledge of minority business
— Seen as not supportive of minority business efforts
— Has big influence on other executives

Max Albert
— African American entrepreneur
— Well known and respected
— Guest of the group

"They're right. It's all our faults," said Don Dressel, gesturing around the table to include the other CEOs in his comments. Don was the CEO of Jaeton City Bank and had lived in the community for years.

"Because we're doing too much and getting too little in return. I've asked my people to do some research," he said, opening the manila folder in his hand. He looked down and began to read. "We had sixty-one different forums, matchmakers, workshops, award ceremonies, and minority business training sessions over the last year. What did this community get in return on the investment it took to fund those sixty-one events?" He looked up. "Does anyone even have a clue? I don't. And this is the last year I answer that question in this nebulous way. Next time, I will *know* the answer or I'm not signing up to support any of these programs again."

"Don, you may be oversimplifying the situation a bit, but you do have a point," Bob Smithton said. Bob was a CEO people often said "didn't get it" when it came to minority business. Bob leaned forward to continue. "We've been dancing around the facts far too long. It's not popular but it's true. We've been investing and promoting and joining and cajoling and waiting for decades. Why aren't we making more progress?"

"Gentleman, gentlemen, we're not here to answer the questions; we're here to *ask* them," urged Mary Michael, the only female CEO in the room, in a maternal *shame-on-you-boys* manner. "We have a guest in our midst," she continued, looking over at Max Albert. "We asked Max here to help us figure this all out because it feels like we've run out of gas."

An active community leader, Max Albert was 58 years old and, by almost every account, was living the American Dream. He'd been married to Dawn for 32 years and had the ultimate personal trifecta of time, good health, and financial wealth after building and selling his valve manufacturing company. The decision to sell his company was a tough one. Max remembered feeling proud of the business he had built and how he had become connected to it personally. But the financial advantages of selling were too significant to let pass. He was now sure he made the right call selling it when he did. He had known Don, Bob, and Mary for years and was a friend of Wade's. Since Wade moved to town, the two had already worked on a number of community initiatives—one to improve downtown and another to lobby for more state government support for Jaeton City. These two guys just hit it off, their mutual respect evident.

"Well, at least I know the topic and I understand you guys are not real happy right now. Am I missing anything?" Max asked.

"It's not that we're unhappy. It's just that we're concerned about what we see," Mary explained.

Max leaned back in his chair. "Tell me what you're seeing."

"It's like a perfect storm. Our businesses have become more complex. And we need our suppliers to have more reach and scale. We depend on them to make us more competitive. The downturn in the economy has made us focus even more on our suppliers. One approach has been to consolidate them to increase efficiency and to reduce cost," Mary continued. "We asked them to take on more risk so we could take on less. All of this had a mostly negative effect on our diverse suppliers."

"It also doesn't help that we're using fifty-year-old ideas when it comes to growing our minority firms," Max added.

"This economy has been tough on us all," interjected Bob with a glum look.

Max leaned forward again. "Your concerns with minority business didn't happen because of the down economy. This economy has just illuminated the problems we were too busy to solve before. This is a *wake-up call*, not a perfect storm."

No one knew what to say after that. Was Max blaming them too, or just making a comment in general? Noticing their discomfort, he attempted to move the meeting forward.

"I know you guys too well," he said smiling. "You didn't

invite me here to simply express your feelings. What do you need from me?"

"We need your help again, Max," said Don. These business leaders had asked for Max's help a decade ago during racial unrest in their town, and Max had made a difference. His personal success combined with his credibility across racial lines and his passion for Jaeton City made Max a valuable resource.

"My help?"

"Yes! Your help. We know we've made progress, but it appears that progress has stopped. We don't know what's going on right now," Mary stated.

"Even more, we don't know what to do about it. Every proposal we hear sounds like a reconstituted version of activity we're doing now," Wade continued. "I'm not sure anyone knows what will actually work, but everyone's afraid not to do *something*. That seems like a stupid reason to continue doing the same things."

Max had to agree. *Just because we always have, doesn't mean we always should.* "Okay," he said aloud, "I'm beginning to understand your concerns. But what, specifically, do you want me to do?"

"Tell us the answers," Mary said in a matter-of-fact way.

Max smiled again.

Don jumped in. "We trust you, Max, and most people in the community do, too. You're objective. You understand the nuances of minority business. We don't have a scope of work or actual specifications for you to follow. We're coming to you to understand this issue and determine what our organizations can do to improve results."

Bob could barely contain himself as he added, "The PR game is over, Max. The social context of minority business development is holding us back. Either our efforts are about business and getting results or they're not. My organization is close to checking out of this minority business game, and I'd guess doing that might give others the license to stop trying too."

"Max, we realize we're putting you in the middle again," Mary said with knowing concern. Max smiled slightly but didn't speak.

"Offering simple solutions to complex problems has to end," she continued. "If the problems were simply about access, training, and capital, we would have solved them by now. In fact, we're getting signs that we're headed in the *other* direction. Let's face it. This issue is more complex than black or white."

"Max, you know you'll have all the resources you need. We just need you to say 'yes,'" Wade concluded.

"Give me a few days," Max responded. "I want to think it through and be sure I can add something here. How does that sound?"

Everyone around the table nodded in agreement. "Give me a call when you have an answer and we can go from there," Mary said.

Max nodded. "Will do."

CHAPTER
5

WHY SUPPORT
MINORITY BUSINESS?

Max and Wade walked together toward the area where they'd both parked. As the men arrived at their cars, Wade broke from their chit chat about baseball.

"Max, I need to ask you to do something for me."

"Sure. What is it, Wade?"

"If you decide to take this on, help us answer the question of *why* the development of minority businesses is so important," Wade requested. "I understand why childhood obesity is a problem. I'm clear about why we need to fix our public education system. Diversity in the workplace is an imperative for our corporation to attract and retain top talent. I get that. We have always been supportive of the idea of minority business development, but I think we've forgotten the tangible reasons why. Sure, we can spout stuff about it being 'good business' and 'reflective of our customers' and a whole host of other things, but we don't spend time building a business case to support investing in minority businesses *development*. Yet the answer to this question is critical if we plan to get these business leaders to recommit."

Max nodded his head as he pondered Wade's point. He knew he was right. Most of the time, the conversation starts with *what* people should be doing and skips over *why* they should be doing it.

"But there are really two questions, Wade. One is why it's important, and the other is why you and your peers should support it," Max said.

"I agree. 'What's in it for us' addresses the short-term benefits we get from supporting minority business development. Those are important to us because, although we like to say we have a long-term view, it gets easier to consider the long term when we have some short-term incentives," Wade admitted.

"Wade, communities won't be competitive without having a cross-section of the residents engaged in successful entrepreneurship. There will be no way for the community to support itself."

This time Wade didn't respond. Given the strong way he stated this, Max seemed so confident and sure.

"Think about it," Max continued. "Our community is led by major organizations such as yours, but it's supported by our core of locally based, privately held businesses. Their CEOs are typically from the local area, and they don't move their headquarters to other states. Clearly, *their* interests are local. Overall, these privately held firms form the heart and soul of our community."

"Okay, but I don't see why this makes minority businesses so important," Wade said.

"I'll give you a few reasons. First, the demographics alone tell you minorities are an increasing part of our population. If we can't get that growing portion of our population engaged in entrepreneurship, we'll have fewer chances of growing significant firms that are privately held in our community."

Wade nodded his understanding.

"You are chairing the United Way Campaign next year, right?" Wade nodded yes. "Did you know I chaired the campaign a few years back?" Max asked to set up the point he wanted to make.

"And I heard you did a fine job," Wade said smiling.

"That's not why I'm bringing it up," Max said returning the smile. "During that year, the campaign brought in more new minority contributors than in any single year before. Many of those new contributors will give to the United Way for years. I hope you'd agree that's good for our community."

"Of course it is," Wade responded.

"And why was I asked to chair the campaign? Why did I have the time, relationships, and financial resources to say yes?" Max asked.

"Because you ran a successful business," Wade conceded.

"Exactly. But this example isn't about *me*. It's about the power of successful enterprise. Our community thrives today because of wealth created in previous generations. If we plan to be a thriving community in the future, the next generation of wealth will have to come from a more diverse group of people."

Wade understood Max's point but wasn't sure his peers would.

"Wade, so many promises have been made about what minority business development would do, I'm not surprised people stopped believing there's any real benefit. We've been pushing minority business based on its potential for social impact. You've heard what they say: 'Minority businesses will employ the unemployed, save troubled neighborhoods, heal racial tensions, and even reduce crime.' Those reasons might hold an element of truth, but that's *not* what minority business is about. The biggest upside is to create diverse wealth because *having diverse wealth* is the only way to have a thriving community."

"So you're saying this is all about wealth creation for minority businesses?" Wade asked.

"Not every business will generate wealth, but full participation by all segments of the community leads to increased opportunities for wealth creation. And communities thrive on the *spillage* of wealth. Communities want as many thriving privately held companies in their regions as they can get," Max said.

"So the pitch is to support minority businesses getting wealthy?"

"Now you know why people don't tell the truth," Max said with a big grin. "It's much easier to sell the idea that a growing minority business will employ the unemployed. *That* social motivation makes for an easier sales pitch. Instead, what we want is an environment that allows *all* entrepreneurs, regardless of their race, to reach their full capabilities. And yes, for some, that will mean achieving wealth."

"I see you've given this question some thought," Wade commented.

"Yes I have . . . for many years. It's just a tough story to tell so others understand. People will gladly help the poor and the needy, but it seems less than logical to help a group of people reach their potential and maybe even get rich," added Max.

"Except when they're developers or investment bankers or other such professionals. We haven't had a problem creating an environment for them to thrive and prosper," Wade responded.

Max smiled. "Sounds like you're thinking about this question too."

"That's why it's important to the community," he said, reminding Max there are really two questions. "What's the business case for our organizations to support minority business development? To me, some of the benefits are obvious—like social responsibility and all of the goodwill benefits that go along with being seen as a good corporate citizen."

"Wade, the challenge of all business cases is they require a set of assumptions and beliefs. Those assumptions and beliefs can always be refuted, therefore, every business case can be refuted. For example, some organizations believe that ensuring their supply base is diverse also ensures they have suppliers with the best mix of value and cost. The argument is 'how can you be sure you have the best if you haven't sought to include all capable suppliers?' That's their business case.

"Other major organizations base their business case on an opportunity to get more business. Many of them have customers who put criteria to work with minority businesses in their requests for proposal. Doing business with minority firms therefore makes the organizations more competitive in winning the opportunities they seek. To them, their efforts in working with minority businesses are similar to their efforts in making quality improvements and meeting safety expectations. So getting more business *is* their business case."

Wade was following along, connecting what Max was saying with his own business and its opportunities to build a business case. He'd heard much of this before, but combining it with clarifying the benefits to the community gave him confidence that the others might find enough motivation to recommit.

Still, he hesitated. "What about those business owners who still say 'it doesn't matter'?" Wade asked. "Many of my peers have a narrow view. To them, any effort that doesn't lead to gaining more customers doesn't matter."

"Well, the best value and cost business case I mentioned earlier works for every organization; that's universal. And so are the benefits of social responsibility," Max said, pausing to collect his thoughts.

"You know," he continued, "I laugh when I hear people trying to tie 'doing business with minority firms' with business outcomes like increasing market share."

"What's so funny about that?" Wade asked.

"It's funny because the money they spend on minority business development is pennies compared to the amount they spend on other things they can't tie to increases in market share either. As I said, every business case is built based on beliefs and assumptions. As a decision maker, I can justify myself into or out of making whatever selection I want."

Max's comments caused Wade to replay the conversations he had engaged in with his own executives. Max was right. Recently, he'd seen a business case in which a company justified its sponsorship of a race car based on increased customer awareness. The case was full of assumptions and placed value on intangible outcomes. Wade shook his head.

"Great conversation, Max. I've held you long enough. I hope you decide to take this on. We could use your insight," Wade said, shaking Max's hand.

"I'm thinking hard about it," Max replied.

* * *

After Wade left, Max reached for his phone and dialed a familiar number he hadn't called for some time. He needed practical advice and Hugh Belden was his best source. After Hugh heard the gist of what was on Max's mind, he invited Max to meet in their usual spot in Monument Park. Max buckled his seat belt and started on his way.

CHAPTER
6

CONNECTING EFFORT
TO OUTCOMES

A community guy, Max Albert believed it was his duty to give back to the people and the place that had supported his success. He knew he was often asked to get involved because he was black—a fact that had never bothered him. What Max cared most about was whether his involvement could make a difference.

Hugh was the best at helping people gain objectivity on issues. *Sometimes more than I want,* Max thought as he pulled into a parking spot just inside the park entrance. He quickly loosened his tie, rolled up the sleeves of his shirt, and started his way down the walking path.

He could see Hugh, a small, neatly dressed black man, sitting on the park bench half way down the path. Max didn't know much about him, just that he had been an extremely successful entrepreneur and had a way of making others think deeply. Max couldn't help but notice how good Hugh looked, no signs of aging. As he approached,

Hugh didn't look up. Instead, he concentrated on feeding the robins and watching the ducks as they glided down the nearby stream.

Hugh greeted Max by saying, "Have a seat, young man." Hugh was the only person left on the planet who called Max "young man." And it always worked. He actually felt younger every time Hugh said it. Max sat down without saying a word.

Finally breaking the silence, Max said, "The CEOs are frustrated. They see themselves as investing and investing and trying and trying, and their progress appears so limited."

"Do you believe they understand?" Hugh asked.

"Understand what?"

"Do you still work out, Max?" Hugh said seemingly changing the subject.

Max had no idea what his workouts had to do with this issue, but he'd long ago learned to follow Hugh's lead. It typically came around to something meaningful.

"Yes, I do," Max replied. "Why do you ask?"

"What the CEOs are experiencing is similar to what many long-time exercisers experience," Hugh suggested.

"Oh really?" Max said with a smile. "You're going to have to take me through that, Hugh."

"I'll be glad to. I'm not talking about the New Year's resolution crowd. Those people who decide every year this is the year to get into shape, only to quit three months later. I'm talking about the people who've worked out so long, it's become a habit. They're regulars, almost religious about getting in their exercise. They go to the same aerobics classes, use the same treadmills, and follow the same circuit of weight machines."

Max was still lost, but he loved the way Hugh weaved a story together.

"Why do people work out, Max?"

"A lot of reasons—some to lose weight, others to improve their health," he responded.

"You're right. But for many people, once working out becomes a habit, the *act* of working out becomes the goal in place of the two outcomes you just mentioned."

Max was still catching up but beginning to get Hugh's point.

"You may have seen these habitual exercisers. They're in the gym frequently using the equipment while reading a magazine or talking with a friend."

"You're not saying there's something wrong with that, are you?" Max asked.

"No. Of course not. Habitual exercisers show up for reasons that have nothing to do with their fitness. Some connect

41

with their friends. Others enjoy being seen. Many just like to be able to say they worked out. There's nothing wrong with any of those reasons. Who are we to judge? And no matter how little they're actually exercising, what they do accomplish is better than nothing."

"So if it's not a problem, what are you saying?" Max asked.

"I'm saying these exercisers shouldn't get frustrated if they don't see results from their 'workouts.' They can't complain that they're no longer losing weight or increasing strength. Like I said, there's nothing *wrong* with the act of working out. But for many habitual exercisers, working out has stopped being meaningful, at least as it relates to improving results or achieving outcomes. Their workouts could be more meaningful if they were more *connected*."

"Connected?" Max asked.

"A connection of *what* they do, *why* they do it, *how* they do it, and most important, the *difference* it can make. Outcomes suffer when you lose that connection."

Max didn't say anything. *Hugh took the long way around, but I think I get his point*, he thought. The CEOs are frustrated about what they see as a lack of continued progress in minority business development. *But have their efforts become disconnected from the desired outcomes?* Time and activity make it easy for anyone to lose connection with the desired outcomes. Things like planning, reporting, meeting, and advocating take over and *these actions* become the outcomes. *So has doing business with minority companies become just a habit to these major organizations?*

Max honestly didn't know but feared it had.

"So I guess I have to *sweat*, not just participate, if I want the desired outcomes," Max summarized, looking at Hugh for confirmation.

Hugh shrugged his shoulders and flashed an ironic smile. "Well, it's an idea."

MAKING IT MEANINGFUL
It takes some sweat.

What You Do
(Activity)

Why You Do It
(The Mission)

How You Do It
(The Intensity)

+

=

The Difference You Can Make
(The Outcome)

Hugh shifted in his seat, clearly wanting to say more. Max waited quietly.

"After all of the investments we've made in minority business development, we're finally positioned to get the success we've envisioned. We now have everything we need," Hugh concluded.

"What do we have now that we haven't had in the past?" Max asked.

"Although we don't have as many scalable minority firms as we'd like, we do have a critical mass of minority businesses that are larger and with more significant track records than ever before. We have a significant number of capable entre-preneurs of color. Many of them are corporate trained and have serious ongoing industry relationships. And finally, we have more major buying organizations engaged in diversi-fying their supply base. Before this moment, all we could do was treat the symptoms.

"Max, I *believe* there's a reason you're here—and a reason they came to you for help."

Hugh paused to allow Max a chance to absorb what he'd said.

"Remember, Max, we aren't the only community and these aren't the only leaders wrestling with this issue. Virtually every community is struggling with this now—or will be soon. They can't be competitive without finding sus-tainable answers. Plus the leaders in every major buying organization are asking themselves the same questions these executives are asking you.

"Yes," Hugh continued, "this issue *is* bigger than our community. But we do have a secret weapon."

"And that is?"

"You, young man. Everyone will listen to what you have to say because they know you're a thoughtful, balanced, and candid voice—a rare combination. And that's what we need right now."

"That vote of confidence feels good, Hugh, but it also puts me in the middle of a circle of the competing interests among minority entrepreneurs, major buying organizations, and community leaders. Whatever I discover will surely go against what people want to hear. They believe what they believe. It's tough to change their minds."

Hugh just nodded his head. "Well, I'm *not* sure their interests are competing, but I *am* sure your mission is *not* to try to change their minds. It's to help the willing understand what it means to sweat for the outcomes, young man," he concluded as he collected his things. Within moments, he was full into his shuffle down the walking path.

"See you soon, Max," Hugh said as he turned and waved good-bye.

I've grown the company this far but I just can't get over the hump.

CHAPTER 7

IT'S A
<u>DIFFERENT GAME</u>

It had been a few days since Fenton had called Hugh to discuss his business situation. Fenton wasn't surprised when his mentor suggested they meet at his country club. Although he typically met Hugh in the park, they'd also met at the county club where Hugh liked to watch his 15-year-old grandson play tennis. The young man had become quite a player too.

Fenton turned into a parking space, got out of the car, and walked into the club. Hugh stood at the observation window watching two young men play tennis. Fenton took a stance next to him and watched with him.

"It *has* been a while, Fenton. You've got a lot going on. You sounded confused on the phone when you called."

"Yes, I do have a lot going on, Hugh, but I'm not as much confused as I am tired."

"Tired of what?"

"Well, I have a long list. How much time do you have?" Fenton replied giving Hugh a contrary grin. "I'm tired of the rhetoric. I'm tired of running a business that makes me feel like a second-class citizen. I'm tired of the minority business programs being diluted, attacked, and defunded. I'm tired of the negative attitudes coming from just about every direction. I'm tired of pursuing only minority opportunities. I'm just generally tired of it all."

"Well, you can probably add *frustrated* to your description, based on how you sound," Hugh teased. He smiled as a way to slow down Fenton's diatribe. Then he asked, "What brought all this on?"

"I just left my Roundtable meeting and it was like we'd stepped back into the seventies. The blame game was rampant. Us versus Them. And one of the business owners in our group has been struggling so long, it looks like he'll have to close the doors. Of course, you never know the complete story, but he blamed his failure on a contract he lost with PPC Global. And then we heard that the top CEOs in Jaeton City are thinking about withdrawing their support for minority business programs. You know, sometimes I question just how far we've actually come."

"Fenton, overall do *you* believe we've made progress developing minority businesses around here?"

Fenton paused before answering. "Yes, of course we have. But are we making progress now? Or are we just trying *not* to lose the gains we've already made?" questioned Fenton as he turned toward Hugh in frustration.

"Everything comes to a crossroads, Fenton. Minority business development, supplier diversity, economic inclusion—whatever you call it—is simply at a crossroads. The frustration you feel and the questioning you hear always happens when a system goes through a challenge like this one," Hugh said, casting a compassionate look Fenton's way.

"Hugh, I'm simply not motivated to keep going the way I've been going. It's like someone keeps turning up the speed on my treadmill. I'm running faster and working harder but still getting nowhere. I can't keep this up, but I'm not sure what else to do."

"What's changed, Fenton? There was a time you were upbeat and hopeful about the future of your business."

"I just can't get over the hump, Hugh. I've grown the company this far, but now the major buying organizations seem less interested in doing business with us than before. Their interest in diversifying their supply base seems like window dressing, not a sincere desire to do business with us. It's just changing, Hugh," Fenton said, almost sounding defeated.

Hugh had been listening intently and nodded his head, indicating he understood.

The men watched the tennis match in silence. Fenton didn't recognize either player so he finally asked, "Hugh, where's your grandson?"

"We're not here to see my grandson, Fenton. You see that player in the far court?" Hugh pointed. Fenton nodded.

"That's Tim. He started his tennis career like most tennis players who have professional aspirations. He wanted to be a singles champion. As time went on, he realized he had a *better* chance to win as a doubles player so he took that route," Hugh explained.

"How'd that work for him?" Fenton asked.

"It worked well. He and his doubles partner won seven straight regional titles. Tim never quite felt fulfilled because he really wanted to play singles, but he was winning so he stayed with it. Then his partner developed other interests and dropped his serious commitment to tennis. Although they still play together from time to time, his partner supports him differently now."

Fenton was listening to Hugh while watching Tim on the court. He tried to figure out why Tim played so awkwardly, not like a championship tennis player at all.

"So Hugh, how did Tim end up here right now?"

"He went back to reclaim his original dream of being a singles champion."

"He seems to have a long way to go. He's getting thrashed right now," Fenton said with an empathetic grin.

"Whether he has a long way to go or has come a long way already really isn't relevant. The point is *he understands he's playing a different game.* He had played the game for years knowing his partner was around to help, so he didn't develop skills he needed to compete in singles tennis. For example, his lateral movement needs a lot of work. His ability to move backward to address a ball is limited. Even the strategies he uses when playing matches has to change."

Fenton nodded. "I bet he's frustrated."

"Yes, but he also knows he can learn and develop everything he needs. His limitations aren't due to a lack of ability. He's only limited because he hasn't done those things before. There are no secrets to what it takes to play singles tennis. And although his hard work can't guarantee he'll one day be a champion again, it does put him in the game he wants to play."

What's going through Tim's mind right now? Fenton wondered, still watching the action on the court. *How is he facing such a daunting challenge? It must be tough.*

"Fenton, things have changed for you, too," Hugh shifted the subject. "Do you also understand why they've changed?"

Fenton realized all the things that came to his mind were the same old finger-pointing reasons people used. He also realized Hugh wouldn't buy any of those excuses. The truth was he could only understand things from his perspective *and* he hadn't made the effort to understand any other view.

"It all depends on what you want, Fenton. If you want to make a point or find fault in what others *aren't* doing, you're on the right track. But if you're trying to grow your business, you need to understand a few things. When you *understand* the others' perspectives, you will *know* what the changes demand of you."

So I'm playing singles tennis now, aren't I? Fenton thought as the message Hugh was conveying finally sunk in. *The game has changed and I have to be different.*

Hugh patted Fenton's shoulder and gathered his things to leave.

"Fenton, everyone thinks opportunity is as clear as black and white. It's not. It's many shades of gray," Hugh concluded as he walked away. Then he stopped and snapped his fingers as if he had just remembered something important. "When you really want to understand other perspectives, give Max Albert a call. He's working on something that might interest you. But don't call him until you're ready." Hugh shuffled his way down the hall and out of Fenton's sight.

* * *

Fenton turned back and stared at the two tennis players a while longer. Although Tim was far from championship ready, Fenton could feel his determination. Just as he was about to leave, he noticed a folded sheet of paper on the ledge of the observation window. He picked it up. "The Answer Is Shades of Gray," he read. He immediately looked around for Hugh who'd already gone. *Was it Hugh who left this piece of paper?*

Fenton shook his head as he refolded the piece of paper and tucked it into his portfolio. *Hugh never stops teaching does he.*

CHAPTER
8

THE BANK IS BACK
TO THE BASICS

It had been almost a week since Fenton had received the call from Ralph Blaine at Jaeton City Bank. Since then, he couldn't stop worrying about his line of credit.

As he walked into the bank's main entrance, a young man greeted him in the lobby and escorted him to a small conference room along the outside wall of a large common area divided into cubicles. Fenton always felt nervous when it came time to renew his firm's line of credit. Access to this capital was the oxygen of his business. He didn't think his managers abused the line of credit, but they did actively use it. It covered expenses while they waited on receivables. It smoothed out the slow periods and helped when the unexpected happened. And, of course, the unexpected always happened.

Ralph Blaine walked into the conference room first, followed by a woman Fenton had never met.

"Fenton, this is Meg Weil. She leads our middle market group here at the bank. I thought it would be good if she sat in on our conversation," Ralph explained.

This can't be good. Ralph had never needed anyone with him before, Fenton thought.

After they went through the formalities of greeting each other, Ralph started the conversation. "Well, Fenton, thanks for coming in," he said, looking up from the papers in front of him. He wanted to get straight down to business. "We've evaluated your application to renew your company's line of credit. Your package was complete and we always appreciate that," he said with a hint of discomfort. "Fenton, you've been a valuable customer with us for years, but we need to tell you we have some concerns with renewing your line."

Fenton's heart sank. He'd had no problem renewing his line in more than 10 years. "Oh really," he responded as calmly as he could. "What types of concerns do you have?

"Well, the bank looks at deals differently these days. And the trends we see with your business concern us."

"Okay. Take me through your concerns."

Ralph reached for one of the papers. "First, your revenue is flat and hasn't grown much in four years. Your profit margins get smaller every year. Add that to your increasing general and administrative expenses, and your net profit is eroding. Frankly, we're not sure you can service this level of debt going forward."

Fenton strained to listen without becoming defensive.

"And Fenton, seventy percent of your sales are with one company. That's just more risk than we like to take these days. Anything can happen with that relationship and, if it did, your business would be in a vulnerable position."

"Ralph, I'm not sure I understand what's changed from your perspective. Our firm remains profitable. Our business continues to have strong contracts with significant customers. We've always managed our credit line well. The concerns you mentioned aren't new, plus they're reflective of the trends in the type of work we do."

Meg jumped in. "Mr. Rice, it's just how we're looking at businesses these days. We're not saying you're doing something wrong. We just need you to know how we're evaluating your business and, at the same time, how we're looking at risk in our portfolio. We still value you as a customer. We simply need to find an alternative way to get you the type of credit you need."

"So you're saying you're not going to renew our line of credit?" Fenton asked abruptly, pushing Meg to clarify her last statement.

"We simply can't renew it at the current level and with the current terms," Meg replied in a firm manner clearly not shaken by Fenton's tone. "Ralph will work with you to see what else we can do to meet your needs. I asked to sit in because I wanted to meet you and to express my support for your business," she said as she stood up. "Mr. Rice, we respect how you've grown your company. We want to continue to be your bank, but we're trying to be as transparent as we can. Things are just different now," she concluded in a conciliatory way, reaching out her hand to Fenton. "Ralph is one of our best. No one in this bank knows your business better. Work with him and I'm confident we can find the right banking solution to meet your needs."

Fenton stood up to shake her hand and thanked her for her time, then Ralph and Fenton sat back down. Fenton leaned forward, eager to know more.

"What's really going on, Ralph?"

"I tried to warn you, Fenton."

Ralph was right. He had tried to alert him to the warning signs he was seeing, but Fenton had taken no action. The bank had always renewed his line of credit and Fenton believed it always would.

"Things really are changing around here. We're looking at our portfolio of privately held firms differently than in the past because things have changed for us too. New regulations. The wave of bank failures. All of it has made us rethink how we perceive risk."

"You *know* us, Ralph. You know where we've been. You know how we respond. We have outstanding contracts with outstanding customers. Now that's become a problem?" Fenton tapped the table with his finger as he made each point.

"Having outstanding contracts with great customers is never a problem, Fenton. It's your concentration with one customer, your decreasing gross margins, and your increasing expenses. *Those* are the problems."

Fenton opened his mouth to speak, but Ralph cut him off. "I know what you're going to tell me, Fenton. You have multiple relationships in different divisions of the same company. We've been through this discussion before. That matters, but not all that much. If that customer changes its purchasing policies or is acquired by a competitor or has a significant downturn in business, any one of these things could affect the amount of business you do with the company.

"Fenton, let's face it. You guys run a very good company, but you don't do anything many other suppliers couldn't do. That leaves you vulnerable."

Fenton could feel himself taking the words personally, so he decided to offer no defense. Instead, he asked for more clarification.

"So what does this all mean, Ralph? My line of credit is due for renewal in sixty days. Exactly what's your bank telling me?"

"Honestly, my management wanted to tell you no, but our history with you gave me the opportunity to get them to compromise. So here's the deal. Come back in the next thirty days with a strategy to accomplish three things: get the business growing again, diversify your customer base, and improve your profit margins. If you can present a plan that makes sense, I think we can get them to renew your line—at least on a provisional basis.

Fenton pulled a piece of paper from his leather portfolio and wrote a few notes. "Is that it, Ralph?" he asked, trying to show no emotion.

"Fenton, I have to tell you this. Any renewal will be based on our history with you and the new *promise* you make with the plan you present. But next year, it will be only about your business performance. Plans and promises won't help next time."

Fenton understood. He focused on containing his disappointment with the bank, with Ralph, and most of all with himself. *How had he let this happen to his company?* Republic was constantly asking for lower and lower prices. But what choice did he have? He either had to deliver lower prices or someone else would. And deep down, he knew his firm would be out of business if Republic walked away as a customer. He also knew better than to let one company become such a high percentage of revenue, but he'd slipped into a rhythm. It was easier to get more work from Republic than to attract new customers. Now he was forced to address the situation. He was stuck in a tough spot given the needs of his business, the pressure of a demanding customer, and bankers who didn't like what they were seeing.

* * *

Fenton and Ralph talked for a few more minutes and agreed on a timeframe for their next meeting. Fenton rose to leave the conference room. Ralph shook his hand and Fenton headed to his car. Once he got in, he let out a deep sigh. "Man," he said aloud. Feels like the world is trying to tell me something. *But what*, he thought. Fenton started the engine and headed back to his office to talk this through with those in his management team. They were expecting him, and they had a lot to talk about.

CHAPTER
9

THE THREE FACES OF
SUPPLIER DIVERSITY

It had been almost two months since Max told the CEO group that he would take on the effort they'd requested. He'd spent that time interviewing executives and professionals from major organizations as well as minority business owners. He also reviewed dozens of studies, surveys, evaluations, and reports, and talked to professional consultants in minority business development. He sat in on small group discussions and met with 11 different community groups.

Clearly, Max was getting a robust view of how buying organizations were working with minority suppliers. His research led to a deep understanding of what was driving the current frustration and perceived lack of progress. The CEOs said they needed his candor and objectivity. Max would take that request seriously.

In terms of being accountable to the CEO group, Mary Michael had volunteered to be Max's main contact. Sitting in her expansive office to discuss his findings, Max looked out the windows that lined an entire wall and showed off a view of the river. *How breathtaking*, he thought.

Mary's welcoming demeanor made him feel comfortable enough to joke with her. "Mary, remind me to thank you for such an interesting opportunity," Max said in a pleasant but teasingly sarcastic tone.

She smiled in response. "Max, you know you love this opportunity. So tell me what you've found out so far."

He smiled, knowing she was more right than wrong. "Well, I've spent the last several weeks *understanding* the environment. At first, I felt confused about some of the tactics being deployed and the metrics being used by major buying organizations. But after I had enough conversations, listened to enough presentations, and then tied together what I was hearing with what I was seeing, the picture became clearer."

"So what's the picture?" Mary asked, wanting to get right to the point.

"Here's what has helped me structure my thinking about the current makeup of supplier diversity," Max continued as he slid a piece of paper across the table to her. "I've started calling it the Three Faces of Supplier Diversity. That is, how things *look*, how they *feel*, and how they *are*. Supplier diversity programs are constantly balancing these three faces."

THE THREE FACES OF SUPPLIER DIVERSITY

1. How It Looks

2. How It Feels

3. How It Is

Mary nodded that she followed him so far.

"These three faces determine everything," he continued. "They make the people involved either more hopeful about their impact or they don't. These three faces enable the systems, metrics, and activities . . . or they don't."

"I don't understand why the three faces are so important," Mary admitted.

"The three faces help the people in the process believe in what they're doing," Max replied as he leaned away from the paper to collect the right words of explanation. "Internally, managing the three faces well contributes to a higher level of personal commitment. It creates a sense of purpose and pride. Managed poorly, these elements lead to feelings of hypocrisy and frustration within a company.

"And the same thing happens with external stakeholders," continued Max earnestly. "Minority business owners see more opportunity, pursue it more effectively, and are more likely to become competitive diverse suppliers. When the three faces are managed effectively people will gain or lose confidence, see or not see opportunity, embrace or not embrace the mission—all based on their interpretation of these three faces."

"Ok, I get the concept and it does provide a good framework. I see how the three faces directly affect our success. But what's your point?" Mary asked bluntly.

"The point is we've gotten these 'faces' out of balance. How any efforts working with minority businesses *look* has become more important than either how things *feel* or how they *are*. "

"Do you really think that's true?" Mary asked.

"The evidence suggests it is," Max responded. "Probably the best example is how the practice of spending targets has taken on a life of its own. The concept of establishing a target for minority spending is probably the cornerstone of much of our progress. That's good. But then the spending target replaced the real goal of developing competitive, wealth-creating minority enterprises," Max explained, holding his hands to the side as he made the point.

"So instead of spending targets being used as a means to grow competitive diverse suppliers, they have become the goal itself," Mary offered.

"Yes. An organization's level of spending is easy to communicate, so it's a perfect way to affect how things *look*. Over time, then, working the system to reach the spending targets became the activity," Max explained.

"Your term 'working the system' seems extreme, Max." Mary shifted uneasily in her large, brown leather chair.

"Maybe a little. But have you seen the measures some organizations and suppliers take to drive up their level of diverse spending? *Extreme* is the only way I can describe it. It's good to want to reach the spending target, but it's as if people think this is a video game and their mission is to score points," Max said. His raised voice showed how passionately he felt about this issue.

"Max, I thought we wanted people to have spending targets, and I thought you would welcome organizations and suppliers going to 'extremes' to reach those goals. Now I'm confused. What *do* you want?"

"Mary, that's a great question. To make progress, we need our activities to impact the outcomes we want. It's a lot like how you might approach exercise. If you measure your success based on frequency and length of stay at the gym, going there often and spending a long time during each visit gives you a high score. And although we know both frequency and duration are factors in reaching your fitness goals, they don't necessarily mean you'll be healthier. Going often and staying long doesn't necessarily mean you lower your blood pressure, improve strength, or lose weight. You have to work up a sweat to get the outcomes you want," he concluded. He could hear Hugh's words echoing in his ear as he spoke.

"That means having spending goals doesn't necessarily yield sustainable, competitive minority suppliers. So you're saying our efforts have to be more *connected* to the desired outcomes, right?" Mary clarified, demonstrating her new understanding.

"Yes, and to do that it takes a balance of all three of the faces because that balance drives the type of activity—focused on the right mission and with the right level of intensity—to create the outcomes we want.

"Mary, the sensitivity to how things look also limits our progress because we don't want to lose any of the 'numerical' ground we've gained. So, for example, although we realize a joint venture we've helped form isn't creating a business that's sustainable, we keep doing business that way because it boosts our numbers. Internally, our people are given incentives to focus on the spending goal but not the *ultimate* goal, which is creating competitive diverse suppliers."

"Max, I'm not sure I followed that. Are you telling me some of our minority spending isn't *real?*" she asked, showing her concern.

"I hesitate to say it's not real, but much of that type of activity simply *won't* create the kind of minority business environment we all say we want," Max replied.

"Oooooookay," Mary said, thinking through how she should respond. "It's no secret that major organizations want to be seen as good corporate citizens. There's nothing wrong with that."

"Not a thing. And thank God they do. Their corporate citizenship is the source of many great things in our community in general and specifically in minority business development. How things look is important; we just have to manage the other two faces of supplier diversity, too, so they're all in balance."

Mary was beginning to understand the need for the balance Max was suggesting. Together, they went through the rest of Max's findings and she asked clarifying questions. He made it clear he'd also have specific recommendations for the group.

As their meeting ended, she asked Max to get input from Bob Smithton before making a presentation to the entire CEO group. "You know he can be a tough personality," she emphasized. "I don't want him hearing all of this for the first time in our group meeting."

Max and Mary both stood up from the conference table.

"The Three Faces of Supplier Diversity," Mary said referring to the paper Max had shared with her. "How it looks.

How it feels. How it is. That alone helps a lot Max. I'll get the meeting with the others scheduled."

"And I'll get a meeting set up with Bob in the next few days," Max confirmed.

CHAPTER
10

THE CAPACITY
TO SUCCEED

Fenton got up early and had already driven halfway to his office by 5:00 a.m. He had a lot on his mind. He and his management team had been meeting almost constantly for a week, plotting the future course of the company. But they weren't getting very far. They just kept coming up with strategies that were no different than what they'd always done. So he decided to drive to his office early and spend some quiet time clearing his busy mind.

The sound of his cell phone ringing seemed odd. *Who would call this early?* He pushed the answer button on his steering wheel.

"Fenton Rice," he said.

"Fenton, this is Carol. Sorry to call you so early, but I wanted to make sure I at least got a message in to you this morning."

Over the years, he and Carol had shared so many important experiences and now she was also a member of the Roundtable. Fenton thought of Carol almost as a sister.

"What's going on, Carol?"

"I'm calling to ask *you* that. I know you've got a lot going on with the bank situation and losing your vice president of operations. I haven't heard from you so I'm calling to check in."

"It's been an interesting time, that's for sure. Things seem to be slipping backward. Or maybe it's more accurate to say that everything is moving forward except our business. I don't think we're any worse or any less capable, but we're still having trouble staying competitive."

"I've never heard it stated that way before," Carol replied, "but that's the picture I'm seeing more and more, particularly with minority firms. A lot of this change started during my last few years running supplier diversity at Republic. The firms aren't any worse, but the world has gotten more competitive and major buying organizations have slowly changed their approach to diverse suppliers. The combination is catching many firms without the capacity to succeed," Carol explained.

"The capacity to succeed. Hmmm." Fenton paused. "What do you mean, the capacity to succeed? Is it any different than the capacity building we've talked about for years?"

"Yes. I'm not sure what we've been building, but it's not capacity," Carol answered. "We use the term 'capacity building' so often, I think people have stopped asking what it means. Training courses on things such as Six Sigma and LEED provide great exposure, but they're seldom enough to add to a firm's capacity. Plus the biggest focus has been solely on the capacity to do work, produce product, or provide a service. It's a definition based on how much activity a business can drive through without blowing it."

"Right. That's how I've always understood capacity."

"Well, that's an important component of capacity but focusing on just the *do work* part of capacity is a trap."

"How so?"

"Answer me this, Fenton. How important is the amount of work you can do if you can't get the work and you can't make any money doing the work? The definition of the *capacity to succeed* is a combination of being able to get work, do work, and get paid. Not one of these is more important than the others."

"Hmmmm," he mused, his interest piqued. He turned his car into a corner gas station, pulled over, and put the gear shift into park. He knew he couldn't concentrate on what Carol was saying and drive safely, too.

Carol continued, "Successful firms have figured these things out. They have systems, processes, metrics, expectations, resources, and goals for each. Your mission as a business owner is to leverage the supplier diversity and minority business programs but not let them handicap you. It's tricky. The assistance you get is helpful, but it can also unintentionally separate you from the *get work* and the *get paid* elements of the capacity to succeed."

From his leather portfolio, Fenton pulled the old envelope he had used to take notes before. He wanted to make sure he captured what she was sharing. It all made sense, and Fenton could think of many examples of how this had happened to his business.

"You know you're right," Fenton agreed. "When we are brought into an opportunity as a sub-supplier to a prime supplier, we are typically separated from understanding exactly how decision-makers identified the opportunity, sought the business, and secured the contract. We missed the entire *get work* phase."

"Well, not completely. You did have to do something to get the work as the sub. But the *prime* supplier may have been searching for a *minority* sub, which changes the dynamics of how you get work. So at best, it teaches you how to get the work as a minority sub. Consequently, you never grow a market-competitive *get work* element of your capacity to succeed," Carol explained.

"The element of getting paid is a little less clear to me. I assume you mean more than our ability to collect the money that's owed to us, right?" Fenton asked.

"Yes, getting paid is more than just collecting, although collecting your accounts receivable is important. *Getting paid* includes all the things that lead to profit—items such as your ability to price well. How well you do in your bidding, proposing, participating in reverse auctions or any other form of pricing your opportunities are all the beginning of your ability to get paid. But getting paid also includes your ability to continually lower your cost structure, leverage supplier relationships, manage cash flow, manage gross margin, gain economies of scale, add higher margin products, plus an endless list of other items," Carol explained.

None of this was new to Fenton, but he hadn't seen it in this way before. He hadn't put these elements together into the context of capacity to succeed. And he also hadn't understood how minority business programs can unintentionally retard the competitiveness of these three components: get work, do work, get paid.

"Are you suggesting our lack of understanding of the capacity to succeed is why we feel we're losing traction as a business?" he asked Carol. A new angle was creeping into his thinking.

"I'm sure that's part of it," she continued. "No one wants to admit it, but almost all minority firms develop an overdependence on supplier diversity programs. Some start out that way and never change. Others have the best intentions, but the system leads them down that path of least resistance.

"You may also be feeling that way because the landscape has changed over the years. Major buying organizations like Republic and PPC have changed the rules, increased the expectations, and broadened the definitions. The political and practical reality has shifted and the genie isn't going back in the bottle. "

Fenton was impressed. "Get work, do work, and get paid. Carol, you've described a framework to understand what we've been missing. Good stuff!"

"I'm glad I could help. I'm just sharing what I've experienced from the other side."

"Well, just so you know, I'm doing fine. Even better *now*. We'll get through this." His voice has brightened.

"I know you will, Fenton. You always do. As I've said many times, I'm betting on you."

* * *

The two hung up. Fenton took a few moments to finish adding his notes to the back of the envelope. *The Capacity to Succeed: Get Work, Do Work, and Get Paid,* he wrote. *This is what the bank has been trying to tell me,* he thought. *I haven't been successful in getting work from additional customers. And the way our profit margins are slipping, I haven't been doing well at getting paid either.*

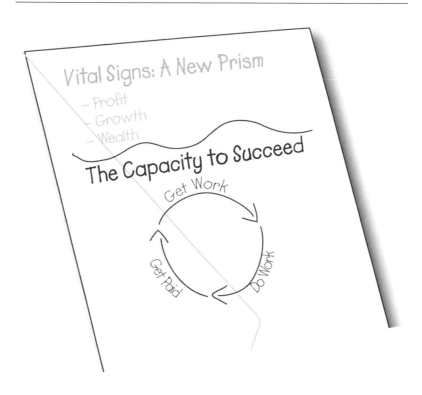

Suddenly his phone vibrated twice indicating he had a new email. He scrolled through to check his message.

"What the heck is this?" he asked as he read the recent email. Then he moved quickly, dialing a number to reach Roger, his manager of field operations. He had to leave a voice mail. "Roger, this is Fenton. I just got an email from a plant manager from our new customer, VisaDial Corporation. It says the company is closing down the site where we have our contract. Didn't we already staff up and invest in preparing for this account? Did you know about this? Help me understand what's going on. I need to know as quickly as possible how this will impact our revenue and profit projections. Thanks."

Although I love the information Carol shared, I just hope I have a business left to use it in. Fenton couldn't avoid the irony. Losing this new customer means Republic would now make up almost 80 percent of his company's total business. "The bank will love *that,*" he mumbled sarcastically.

CHAPTER

11

INTERESTED OR COMMITTED?

His meeting with Mary had been a struggle, but Max felt good about sharing his early findings with her. *If these issues were easy, we would have solved them already*, Max thought as he walked through the hallway of his private club on his way to meet Bob Smithton for lunch. Mary had advised Max to talk with Bob before calling for the group of CEOs to meet. Bob influenced the others in a major way. If he decided against anything, it always became a perfect excuse for the others to do the same. Everyone in the group thought they knew where he stood on this issue—and it wasn't favorable. *Checking Bob's temperature* before the CEOs met would be prudent.

Although Bob and Max had tussled on the Accelerator project, the two gentlemen had respected each other for a long time. Bob was admittedly surprised by how successful that initiative had become. He'd always had strong feelings about how things ought to be; Max knew his attitude in this conversation about minority businesses would be no different. However, engaging Bob in the process would still prove to be more fruitful than not.

"Good afternoon, Mr. Albert," the maître d' greeted Max as he walked into the restaurant. "Your guest is waiting for you in the parlor."

"Thank you," Max replied, and he walked into the parlor. "Greetings, Bob. Thanks for joining me for lunch." They shook hands. "They have a table ready for us. This way."

It didn't take long to order lunch and exchange pleasantries. Although Bob was full of bravado, Max actually appreciated him. Bob was a committed community leader, and he cared deeply about issues. Best of all, people always knew where they stood with him. That's what Max appreciated most.

"Bob, I wanted to make sure I previewed my work with you before we got in front of the other CEOs," Max said, transitioning their casual conversation to the matters at hand.

Before Max could go on, Bob interjected, "I've thought a lot about the minority business issue since our last meeting, Max, and here's what I think."

Okay, Max braced himself. *This is one of those meetings where he takes over my agenda. Not good.*

"We're doing enough already," Bob stated as he buttered his bread. "I'm not spending any more money. I'm not creating any more programs. And I'm not going to ask my people to reach out any further. We've tried. If people can't or won't take advantage of their opportunities, then it's time to move on."

Max could feel himself growing agitated.

"Well, Bob," Max said, collecting himself, "why did you ask me to do this if your mind was already made up?"

"We already know the problems, Max. They haven't changed. I always felt skeptical about asking you to do anything. But since then, I've spent more time looking at our own efforts. In my company, we've shown our interest in minority business development. No one can question that."

"They may not question your interest in it, but I can surely question your commitment to it," Max said, letting his frustration show. "Bob, there's no doubt we've made progress, and if you're saying that's enough for you, great. But don't say you're frustrated that we're not making progress and at the same time *not* be willing to hear why and how we can move forward. Minority business development is at an important crossroads. All the progress has us positioned to move toward entrepreneurial parity. And that's going to take more than your mere *interest*."

Max and Bob often had heated conversations. Max found Bob to be a bit of a bully and believed this tension was the only way to break through with him. The two men sat uncomfortably for what seemed like ages. Then Bob spoke.

"Max, we meet or exceed all of the industry standards for components of a credible supplier diversity program," Bob said, starting to count them off on his fingers. "We keep

77

track of our spending with minority firms, we participate in the various groups and outreach efforts, we sponsor events, we ask our prime suppliers to also do business with minorities, and we set goals for our spending."

"And you often reach your goals, too. Bob, you're right. Your organization has shown interest. But just like your suppliers have to continue to evolve as your needs evolve, your approach to minority business has to evolve, too. I'm not asking you to spend more money or create new programs, man, I'm just asking you to listen. Do you realize that everything you've done shows your *interest* but not necessarily your *commitment*?"

"Oh, really? What do you see as the difference?" Bob asked looking up from his plate. He put down his knife and fork.

"What would you do if it had to happen?"

"If what had to happen?" Bob asked.

"What would you do if you *had* to have success doing business with minority firms? The actions that answer that question are the difference between your interest and your commitment," Max explained taking a sip from his glass of water.

"The difference is when an organization pursues building a base of diverse competitive suppliers in the same way they pursue other things that have to happen in their business," he continued. "You know, how you might attack things such as cost reduction or quality improvements. You assign top talent, create a strategy that holds the organization accountable, and tie performance to evaluations

What would you do if it had to happen?

and compensation. The difference between interest and commitment is when an organization goes from the supplier diversity people *pushing* it through the organization to individuals throughout the organization looking to *pull* minority firms into the supply base."

"That's all much easier said than done, Max. There aren't enough minority firms of the scale and reach that we need. You're not being realistic," Bob responded, dismissing Max's point.

"I get that, Bob, but if we stay on our current course, there never will be enough minority firms that represent the scale you need. There are many reasons why we can't do better. That's not new. There are always reasons for the challenges we face in business. That's what makes them challenging. But the way we deal with the realities accounts for the difference between *interest* and *commitment*," Max said, seeking common ground.

"But we don't *have* to work with diversity suppliers for our businesses to succeed," Bob protested.

"I agree with you again. However, you can't say you don't know how to do more meaningful business with minority firms. You handle this like you handle every other challenge you face."

Bob nodded. "Okay. Although we don't agree, you have my attention, Max. What are you proposing?" He leaned in and put his elbows on the table.

"I propose you come to the meeting with the other CEOs and join me in talking through the things you and I have talked about. I won't propose any new programs or larger budgets. We'll just talk through the realities of our current situation and candidly discuss the difference between interest and commitment. I'll end with a few specific recommendations, and then everyone can then take the information and do with it what works for them. Can I have your agreement on this approach?"

"You do. Hey, I apologize for shutting you down when we first started talking," he offered in a much friendlier tone than earlier. I'm just used to people coming to me and telling me how what I'm doing isn't enough. When they tell me how much more they think we ought to be doing, they rarely have their facts straight. And they can see only their own perspective, no one else's."

"Believe me, I do understand. What's important is that we got to a place where we can both agree."

CHAPTER
12

HOW MUCH VERSUS
HOW MEANINGFUL

Max had been speaking to the group of CEOs for about 30 minutes. He presented why minority business development was so important to the community and the sources for the individual organizations to develop their business case. He spent time explaining what he had talked about with Bob Smithton on the differences between interest and commitment. He reviewed much of what he and Mary had discussed, including the Three Faces of Supplier Diversity. The group had a lot of questions and just as many comments.

"I realize I'm saying a lot," Max responded to their comments. "And you may even believe I'm blaming your organizations for where we are. I'm not. But based on what I found, I'm saying this is our moment. The pace of global change and the new nature of competitive markets have us in a position where we have to reach entrepreneurial parity now or risk never getting there. This is our chance to turn our investment in minority business into the results espoused back in the sixties when Nixon declared the need for minority capitalism."

"So you say you're not blaming us. And you're saying we have a unique moment right now. But exactly what are you telling us to do, Max?" asked Wade Blair.

"I'm suggesting you make your spending with minority owned firms more meaningful."

"Well, I suspect our spending is already meaningful for the businesses who get it," quipped Bob.

"Of course it is," Max agreed. "But it can be even more meaningful for our mutual benefit of growing the number, scale and sustainability of minority enterprises."

"Our spending is doing that now, Max," refuted Don Dressel of Jaeton City Bank. "I meet these business owners every day."

"With all of the respect I can muster, I say to you it happens in too few of the cases, Don. Are people thankful to be doing business with you? Yes. Are they building the types of businesses, in the kinds of industries, with the quality of strategies that will one day make minority business programs unnecessary? I can't find any nonbiased source that will say 'yes' to any of those questions. Let's not fool ourselves. What's happening now is generally not sustainable without special programs."

"We have already committed a lot of resources to get the progress we have," Wade added.

"Yes. And what we've been doing is important activity," Max explained.

"Just so we're all clear, when you say activity you mean things like certification, spending goals, outreach events, and providing training opportunities, right?" Bob asked.

"Yes, I do. And things such as mentoring programs and capacity building experiences. All of these efforts have merit. The big opportunity is to continue to do the activities we just listed but focus more on *how* we do them."

"Explain what you mean," said Wade genuinely curious.

Max paused as he searched for the right words.

"So much of *what* we do is because we've always done it or because our peers do it. Other things we do because our customers encourage us to. And sometimes we do things because we don't want to appear to be uninterested in growing minority businesses. Rarely do we engage because we would like to eliminate the need for these programs one day. We're not doing what we're doing to make sure these businesses thrive. We're more focused on our short-term interest than we are on the long-term possibility of mutual interest." Max explained.

"You just can't keep from pushing the blame our way, can you?" accused Don.

"I'm sorry you keep seeing it as blaming. You did ask me to look into the situation and provide candor. Well, this is it. If it's any consolation, you should hear my message for minority businesses. They'll struggle to hear it, too.

"Don, as a community, either we want a new level of progress or we don't. We can't complain about the lack of sustainable success and at the same time defend our current motives and activities. You wouldn't accept that from your executives. I refuse to give that to you here today," Max said emphatically.

"Max is right," Mary said jumping in to stop the back and forth. "We asked him for exactly what he's giving us. What we ultimately do with the information is up to us. " She turned to Max and asked, "How do you propose we pay more attention to *how* we do things? I think we may understand the concepts better if we can hear some examples. Give us the specifics."

"Sure. I'd be glad to." Max turned a few pages in the small stack of papers in front of him. "We have ten specific recommendations organized into three categories. Each is designed to create an environment to make your spending with minority firms more meaningful." He began to read through the list. Number one. Be resolved . . ."

* * *

For the next 50 minutes, Max went through each of the recommendations. The group chimed in to gain clarity. Max thought the conversation was going well. Mary was right. The group was more interested in understanding what they could actually do. He made the point this wasn't as simple as black and white; that it wasn't just *what* they were doing

Recommendations for Committed Major Buying Organizations

1. Be resolved —

- Do it like you do business.
- Don't accept the either/or argument.
- Spread accountability.

2. Be candid —

- Acknowledge internal hurdles.
- Explain the criteria for success.
- Encourage potential.

3. Be bold —

- Avoid the spending goal coup.
- Make inclusion a criterion for suppliers.
- Question majority/minority relationships.
- Increase your expectations for minority suppliers.

See Appendix A for detailed version

that created the opportunity but *how* they were doing it. What to do with what they now understood would be up to them.

By the time he finished speaking, Max was comfortable they at least could understand his perspective on the issue.

Each group member left with a handout of the details behind the information Max had just shared. He said a few final words more as a warning than anything else. "These recommendations will bring more balance to the Three Faces of Supplier Diversity. I present these ideas recognizing that how things *look* is important to your organizations. The recommendations address the importance of how things *feel* and are designed to impact how things really *are*.

"Keep the Three Faces of Supplier Diversity in mind. Think of them when you see the internal reports of your efforts, hear about your organization's performance, and invest in various activities. All three faces are important," Max emphasized. "Balancing the three is the challenge."

CHAPTER 13

ENTREPRENEURIAL PERSPECTIVE

Fenton finally decided to follow through on Hugh's suggestion to call Max Albert. Still feeling uneasy about his firm's future, he believed he and his team were doing the right work to improve things. He was confident at least that they understood their business better. Applying the three components of *the capacity to succeed* had helped bring structure to their thinking.

But Fenton still wasn't sure he understood how the rules of the environment surrounding minority business had changed and how that change was affecting his business. He hoped Max could help him understand it better.

Fenton had heard of Max Albert, but the two had never met. He knew Max was active in the community, well known and respected.

He and Max agreed to meet at the park at 7:00 a.m., Fenton's favorite time of day because the park seemed surreal.

A calm morning mist floated over a small, slow stream yet to awaken from its night sleep.

From a distance, Fenton could see a man sitting on the park bench usually reserved for conversations with Hugh. This man was younger and more casually dressed. He looked to be in his early fifties with salt-and-pepper hair neatly cropped.

"Good morning, Fenton," Max greeted him.

"Good morning, Max. Thank you again for agreeing to meet with me."

"It's the least I can do. Many people have done the same for me over the years. The only payment they asked was for me to do it for others. I'd say I'm getting off cheap. So how can I help?" he asked, turning toward Fenton to give him his undivided attention.

"Max, as I shared with you on the phone, we have a lot of challenges right now. I've got problems with the bank that just got even more difficult. I lost an important vice president right when we needed her most. We recently lost a piece of business with a new customer. No one's fault, but we'd already invested in staff to support it. We're to blame for part of our situation, yet I think some of it reflects the ebbs and flows of business."

Max listened. He had talked to many entrepreneurs and he'd learned that sometimes they just needed to unload.

"Honestly, none of this scares me," Fenton continued. "We'll get through it. I'm proud of my management team. As usual, they've responded like true professionals. But they can only respond with what they know, and it just seems like we're still missing something. We're managing the black-and-white things, but something about the environment has changed."

"Fenton, what you're feeling is what happens as the *era* changes in minority business development. We are moving quickly out of the *Access Era* into the third era I call the *Competitiveness Era*," Max offered.

Fenton remembered the article on the three eras and the fact he had failed to finish reading it. He was suddenly sorry he hadn't gotten it done. "I started reading about the three eras in an article a while ago. I must admit I didn't finish it. Max, were you the author?" Fenton asked.

"I was," Max replied smiling at Fenton's confession. "Fenton, the point wasn't the eras themselves but how the environment for minority business development has evolved. This evolution demands that our thinking change, too. People get stuck with a perspective from one era and are unable to compete in the next."

"Why do you think people aren't responding to the obvious need to change?" Fenton asked.

"Many reasons. Let's face it, although we talk about it, think about it, and even make plans to do it, most of us don't actually change until we *have* to," he replied.

"Max, to be honest with you, I'm not sure I can see another reality for me and my business. I hear the stories about great companies growing and getting funding and the owners becoming wealthy, but I'm not sure I can see my way there."

"Oh, I get what you're saying, Fenton. I was convinced none of that was for me either. I had to make a number of changes to get a more informed vision of success. My *entrepreneurial perspective* was limited by what I understood and what I saw as an actual reality for me."

"That's the right term—*entrepreneurial perspective.* Right now, all I can see is sustaining what I have. But honestly, the effort to do that is starting to become an emotional and financial drain," Fenton said, fatigue clearly showing in his voice.

"Back when I owned my first business, as much as we hated to admit it, our perception of our firm as a minority business limited us. We had to find ways to take those limits off and work to *keep* them off," Max explained.

Fenton still resisted what Max was saying. Was he implying Fenton was to blame for his situation? That's like blaming the victim, isn't it? Was this the old "pull yourself up by your bootstraps" speech?

Max could see Fenton struggling with this idea. "Fenton, forget blame and fault and guilt. I'm just stating the obvious. You have to be able to *see* it before you can possibly *be* it," Max said. "It's 'entrepreneurial perspective'—simply how you see your opportunities. We finally recognized our need to move from being 'outstanding tactical managers of contracts' to 'strategic leaders of an entrepreneurial business.'"

"Hmmmmm. From tactical managers to strategic leaders. That's a big jump. How did you accomplish that?" Fenton asked, his interest piqued.

"It was a process that didn't happen overnight. First, we committed to a continuous flow of new information because we needed a broader view. So we committed to three specific actions. First, we started reading *The Wall Street Journal* every day. The exposure to what was going on kept us current and the stories generated new thinking. We also passed around articles we found interesting. Second, we read three business books throughout the year together as a management team and spent an evening over dinner discussing each book as we finished it. Sometimes we found things we wanted to use in our business and other times we didn't," Max explained.

Fenton had opened his leather portfolio and grabbed a piece of paper for taking notes. This all sounded good, but it also sounded like quite a time commitment.

"We also realized we needed to occasionally get out of the day-to-day grind of running our business. So the last part of our plan to have a continuous flow of new information was going away to some type of multi-day training at least once every twenty-four months."

"That all sounds good, but I'm so busy now, I can't imagine fitting all of that in," Fenton responded.

"You asked me how we *changed* our entrepreneurial perspective. Changing that required us to change our *behavior* too," Max explained, encouraging Fenton to make the connection.

"Okay," Fenton said smiling slightly. "I get it. A continuous flow of new information was first. What was next?"

"Next, we wanted to broaden our entrepreneurial circles. To go from tactical managers to strategic leaders, we had to intentionally build a network of people who had 'been there and done that.' So we looked to join groups comprised of leaders of significant privately held businesses, business investors, entrepreneurs, and bankers. We wanted to be in an environment where business was being discussed and with people who were doing business. Careful to join only a few groups, we kept a low profile until we knew the group fit our needs well."

"Did you see benefits from doing this?" Fenton asked. "Were these people willing to do business with you?"

"Those are two different questions, Fenton," Max pointed out. "Yes, I would say we saw benefits, but our mission was to change our entrepreneurial perspective. In fact, we did business with very few of the people we met through these groups. But as we built stronger relationships, we were exposed to conversations that led to contracts we would never have known about before. Most important, though, our own *perspective* changed."

Fenton was writing and thinking at the same time. He realized that changing his entrepreneurial perspective would take time. He could hear what Max was saying and even see the value, but he wasn't sure it made sense for him. Changing long-held beliefs is always difficult.

"The last step we took was to become students of business models," continued Max. "We questioned everything we saw. . . Why did they create that strategic alliance? What were the elements of value those investors saw in that company? Why did they sell off that division? What opportunity did they see in that acquisition? This process wasn't as specific and structured as the other two activities, but it became addictive. And it really sharpened our skills in seeing opportunities for our business."

Fenton nodded as he took a few more notes. "Sounds like you're saying I've got to change," he said, beginning to fully accept the truth of his situation.

"Or become extinct," Max said with a wide grin. "You always have choices."

* * *

After talking more about business, strategy, and the concept of entrepreneurial perspective, the two men shook hands. Max stood up and left while Fenton lingered, leaning back on the park bench. The sun, now fully up, revealed how the park was showing signs of life. Despite all of his pressing challenges, Fenton couldn't help but feel hopeful about his future and grateful for his relationship with Hugh—and now with Max.

CHAPTER 14

UNDERSTANDING THE THIRD ERA

Before leaving the park, Fenton opened his leather portfolio to review his discussion notes from his conversation with Hugh Belden. As he looked through the papers, he came across the article on the three eras of minority business development and started reading right where he'd left off weeks ago.

> We are at the tail end of the *Access Era* now and moving quickly into what I'm calling the *Competitiveness Era*. The *Competitiveness Era* means more change. Even the organizations most committed to doing business with minority firms will do so with fewer concessions.

THE THREE ERAS OF MINORITY BUSINESS DEVELOPMENT

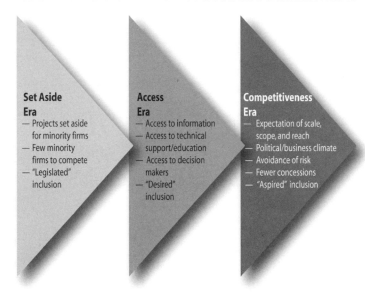

Set Aside Era
— Projects set aside for minority firms
— Few minority firms to compete
— "Legislated" inclusion

Access Era
— Access to information
— Access to technical support/education
— Access to decision makers
— "Desired" inclusion

Competitiveness Era
— Expectation of scale, scope, and reach
— Political/business climate
— Avoidance of risk
— Fewer concessions
— "Aspired" inclusion

What do I mean? I mean the nature of our advanced global market and the changes in how minority business development is viewed has changed the game. Organizations won't go far out of their way to do business with minority firms. They're still interested but they're making fewer and fewer concessions on things like scale, price, reach, or risk. So if your business feels different to you, you're experiencing the impact of these changes in approach that are happening as we speak.

You may be thinking that doesn't seem fair. That's your perspective. What's unfairness in your mind is a business imperative in the minds of major buying organizations. Don't act surprised. There have been warning signs along the way. We've been hearing about the need to be globally competitive for years, but few companies have changed their business model. Using the tactical focus to get the next contract worked for many in the *Access Era,* but it won't work in the *Competitiveness Era*.

Fenton lowered the article to his lap. *The Three Eras of Minority Business Development: The Set Aside Era, the Access Era, and the Competitiveness Era. This explains everything that's been happening,* he thought. *Why didn't someone tell me earlier?* He shook his head and smiled. "I wouldn't have listened anyway."

Fenton reached for his phone and started dialing.

"Michelle, this is Fenton. I think it's time we talk with the entire company. Our people deserve to know where we are and where we're going. Can you take the lead on organizing a companywide meeting in the next few days?"

"Absolutely. That's a great idea, Fenton. They've surely noticed the management team having all of these meetings and you know how rumors can fly. I'll make it happen. Do you have a speech prepared?"

"We've actually been working on my speech for months," he said, reaching in his portfolio for the paper titled *The Answer Is Shades of Gray.* "I'm simply going to share with them what we've learned."

Fenton pushed the end button and leaned back again. He had missed being in the park and how it gave him the room to think. *It's a hot spot for new thinking and new strategies,* he thought smiling.

It speaks to our attitude, our commitment, and our view of our own opportunities.

CHAPTER
15

IT'S A NEW DAY

Fenton and Michelle walked into the large two-story common area in the middle of their office building. Employees filled the first-floor space. Some lined the stairs while others looked down over the rail from the top floor. Fenton needed a microphone to be heard.

"Quite a few of us, aren't there?" Fenton commented to Michelle. "Thanks for putting this together."

"It's easy to forget how big our firm is until you see us all together at one time," she replied. "And just think, they're all waiting to hear from you. . . . No pressure, of course."

"Funny," Fenton replied as he approached the microphone.

"For many of you," he began, "this isn't the first time you've attended a meeting like this. You've been asked to meet new challenges a number of times over our fourteen years in business. Each time, you've responded to the call. I believe in you, and I believe in what we're building together. The question is 'what's next?'

"Our management team has been busy and you'll soon see the results of our planning efforts. For example, we're changing how we decide what contracts to pursue. We're also changing some of our performance metrics to better align with our heightened focus on profitable growth. We'll put more resources toward getting our own projects without relying so much on being a minority participant on the contracts of others."

Fenton reached into his pocket and pulled out the paper he'd found after his meeting with Hugh at the country club.

"All of those changes are important, but I consider them the 'black and white' of doing business. The answer to our future success is not as simple as black and white. It's found in all the shades of gray involved in our approach," Fenton said as he held up the piece of paper.

"A copy of a one-page reminder card titled *The Answer Is Shades of Gray* is being passed out to you right now. The four points on that card remind us that simply doing our jobs is *not* enough. The spirit with which we engage in our jobs matters, too. That becomes both an individual challenge for each one of us and a collective challenge for our organization."

Fenton paused as the cards were being passed around. Once everyone had a copy, he read from the *The Answer Is Shades of Gray* paper he'd held up.

"Number one: See things from other perspectives. We can't get stuck in our own stuff, our own concerns, and our own objectives. We are more open when we can see things the way others are seeing them. We're more open to new ideas, opportunities, and even relationships. There are three sides to every story: ours, theirs and the story we can make work together.

"Number two: Accept challenges as an invitation to be *more*. The effort it takes to overcome challenges fuels the next level of success. Few good things come to us unless we're being challenged. If we aren't being challenged, we're likely not growing. Great companies accept challenges as an invitation to be more.

"Number three: Know the difference between interest and commitment. Our commitment to our own success shows in every element of our business. It shows in our level of preparation, our willingness to study to understand our customers' future needs, and our willingness to improve ourselves as individuals *and* as an organization. 'Interested' means you show up; 'committed' means you show up ready to have a positive impact on the desired outcomes. There's a big difference. To ask someone to be more committed than you are is creating a dynamic that will never produce the results you want.

"Number four: Appreciate that what got us here won't get us there. Situations change. The activities, resources, and attitudes that made us good before will have us left behind in the future. Our clients' needs and expectations evolve, and our business must evolve with them. That has been a fact since the beginning of time. When the environment changes, you must change too or you become extinct."

THE ANSWER IS SHADES OF GRAY

◆ *See things from other perspectives.*

◆ *Accept challenges as an invitation.*

◆ *Know the difference between interest and commitment.*

◆ *Appreciate that what got you here won't get you there.*

Fenton paused and looked around to read how his audience was receiving this message. Hard to tell. At least he could see they were listening intently.

He continued, "The last time we went through a tough patch, our customers demanded that we change. This time, our customers didn't demand it; they simply decided they'd go on without us. Because they can. They used to see it as their responsibility to bring minority-owned businesses along, but that pendulum has swung.

"The good news is we're ready for this change!"

Fenton paused again and looked into the faces of the people in front of him. They looked hopeful but serious. They

102

had it right; the situation was both. He was now speaking to himself as much as he was addressing them.

"I'm taking the Shades of Gray seriously, and I'm encouraging you to do the same. This Shades of Gray piece speaks to our attitude, our commitment, and our view of our own opportunities," he said, placing his hand on his chest. "I got a new lesson this time around. But I promise not to forget it, for there is no *color* of opportunity. The environment is what it is. It's our mission to find the opportunities in it. Thank you all. Let's get back to it."

*If you want to be
one of the best,
do what the best do.*

CHAPTER
16

HOW DO YOU COLOR
YOUR OPPORTUNITY?

F enton looked forward to today's Roundtable meeting. He and his team had finally gained the understanding they needed, and he wanted to share it. They'd done a lot of planning as well as soul searching, and they'd taken several strategic actions over the last several months. In truth, his conversations with Carol, Hugh, and Max had transformed Fenton's perspective. He couldn't speak for anyone else, but he realized he had been operating with a self-imposed glass ceiling on his own entrepreneurial aspirations—partially because he didn't know what was possible and partially because he didn't believe he could have what everyone else could.

As Fenton walked into the meeting, he heard Jimmy describing his experience closing his business and getting into a new joint venture with a majority-owned company. The company's executives thought they could *take advantage* of Jimmy's minority certification in combination with the spending goals of corporations.

Fenton listened hard for signs this venture could prosper in the Competitiveness Era. Not there. *The best he could gain was income and possibly accumulate personal wealth—if he doesn't get shafted first!* thought Fenton. *They're stuck in an old era of minority business development.*

Before long, the group turned to Fenton and asked him to update them on his business activities. Fenton started by stating what he considered to be the most important business question he'd ever been asked.

"My management team and I have been responding to a question I must admit we've never asked ourselves before: *What would we be doing if we weren't a minority-owned firm?* Answering that question has been challenging and even intimidating at times."

"Fenton, I don't understand. Our customers aren't just giving us business. We're doing the work the other suppliers have to do," Maria pointed out.

"You're right. We *are* doing the work the other suppliers are doing and we're doing it well. But that's about the *only* thing we're doing. I want to be clear. Everything I'm saying is about *our* firm and *my* thinking. I'm not suggesting any of this pertains to any of you, although it might. We tried to deny our own reality for a long time until the evidence became overwhelming. What we *weren't* doing was the other stuff necessary to reach our own aspirations. "

"What are your aspirations?" Stu asked, already frustrated with Fenton.

"For us, we realized our dreams weren't big enough or bold enough. Now we're clear we want to build an organization that creates generational wealth. I realized I was taking the risk and doing the work, but I wasn't putting our business in a position to reap the rewards."

"You know I just saw some research that supports what Fenton is saying," Carol offered. "It was only a small study, but it suggested that minority entrepreneurs didn't have as high a level of aspiration for their business as most entrepreneurs do. They wanted to make money but didn't articulate the same opportunity for generational wealth. Personally, I didn't like what the study was saying plus it didn't evaluate why these differences existed. A number of experiences are likely contributing to this reality, but maybe there's some truth to it, too."

"It's not something I want to publicize, but this was true for me," Fenton confessed. "We became over-reliant on the minority business support system. As a result, my aspirations were blocked by the limits I'd placed on the business. I understand that now."

Jimmy grabbed his pen to take notes on the discussion. This got his attention!

Stu spoke up. "I hear you guys, but the reality is we don't have the resources, relationships, and exposure to do what other business owners can do. For an example, I never hear about a company available for me to buy and even if I did, I don't have access to the capital to get the deal done."

"Stu is *right*," agreed John. "We just don't have those networks," he said, putting up his hands as if to push back the idea.

"And if we don't start now, we never will," Fenton emphasized in an understanding but matter-of-fact way. "However, *there are no unavailable resources*. They may just be unavailable to *us*. So making resources available is on our critical path of work that needs to be done."

"This isn't new, guys. We've been talking about it for years," Stu said.

"Then why haven't we done anything about it? Why haven't more of us taken action?" Carol questioned as she looked around the room for responses.

"Probably for a million reasons—some of them psychological, others a matter of focus. But the bottom line is we haven't," Maria admitted. "I know I get so busy with the day-to-day stuff that I just don't have time to be more strategic."

"I think another reason is because our business peers aren't doing it either. Our perspective of opportunities around us is developed by what we see happening. If we want to see how other entrepreneurs are growing successful firms, we'll have to broaden our network of entrepreneurs," Carol added.

"You can try that if you want. But face it—things are just different for minority entrepreneurs," Stu affirmed, stubbornly shaking his head. "They're only going to let you go so far."

"I know things are different for minority entrepreneurs. I'm not naïve to that. I'm just no longer willing to let those differences define the opportunities out there for my business. Some things we just have to get over!" Fenton said.

Clearly everyone at the table didn't appreciate Fenton's

perspective. He realized as much, but he'd decided before the meeting to lay it all out for his fellow Roundtable members. It would be up to them to decide how much of what he said was worthy of their attention.

"You know, I was reading the *Jaeton City Business Weekly* the other day," John said, breaking the ice after Fenton's latest comment. "It featured its annual list of the hundred largest privately held businesses. Most of them were names we've seen on the list for years. But as I read the stories about the eleven new entrants to the list, I noticed they all had a similar theme. They had all grown by an acquisition, merger, or some sort of significant strategic alliance."

"All of them? Did it have something to do with the industry they're in?" Maria asked.

"The industries were all different and none of the companies were spectacular in nature. They were normal block-and-tackle businesses like logistics, construction, packaging, and fulfillment," John confirmed. "I think it was less about their industry than it was about their business activities."

Fenton agreed. "This doesn't mean getting on that list is the entrepreneurial aspiration of everyone, but it's an example of the point. If you want to be one of the best, do what the best do. And we all know growing a sizable business in today's environment is difficult to do one contract at a time."

"We're pretty happy with where we are right now," Stu replied in a way that could have dismissed the entire conversation. "We have good customers. Strong contracts. My wife and I live a nice life. I can't complain and I'm getting what I want."

"And Stu, we should *all* be able to say we're getting what we want," answered Fenton. "But today . . . *I* can't."

* * *

The others continued to talk about their businesses and a few community issues. Jimmy focused on looking through his notes. He knew he'd blown it once before because he'd missed the warning signs about the need to change. And he wasn't about to make the same mistake twice. Maybe the joint venture he was considering didn't make much sense for him—at least not in the structure he was considering.

He read the four items he had written in his notes one by one.

DIARY AND WORK RECORD

Getting my opportunity

1. Be honest and clear about what you want from the business.

2. Don't let race color your opportunity.

3. There are some things we just have to get over.

4. There are no unavailable resources.

CHAPTER
17

WHAT DO YOU UNDERSTAND NOW?

Fenton approached the park bench at Monument Park with a new swagger in his step.

Things weren't where he wanted them to be, but he felt clearer about his direction than ever before. No longer in the business of managing contracts, he saw himself as an entrepreneur. *An entrepreneur with challenges, but an entrepreneur nonetheless,* he thought.

The bankers liked his short-term plan but had only agreed to extend the line of credit for 90-day intervals. *Here we are, three ninety-day extensions later, and they still insist on reviewing the situation every quarter,* he thought. He would have to continue to face that issue. But his activities had changed. And getting together today with Hugh and Max was the highlight of his week.

Max approached the park bench. He wanted to share that his work with the CEOs of the major buying organizations was complete. *Wow, what an experience*, he thought. *Everyone wants change, but no one wants to do anything differently.* The leaders of the community's major buying organizations had a tough time swallowing Max's candor. And when it got down to stating specific recommendations, results were mixed, at best. But Max felt good about the work he'd done and realized it could take years to know if it had actually made a difference.

The two men reached Hugh's bench at about the same time. In a friendly way, Hugh motioned for them both to sit down.

"Well, gentlemen. You two have been very busy. How did it go?"

Max spoke first. "It was an experience, Hugh. My role was to be objective and give the community leaders my best perspective. It was a challenge at times, but all in all, I believe they would say they got what they asked for."

"What about you, Fenton," Hugh asked. "This has been quite a ride for you too."

"Hugh, you've watched me go through this type of situation before, and it's always a roller coaster ride. I guess I don't react until I get into a real tough spot. But I have to tell you, this one changed me. I just see things differently. My new clarity allows me to give clarity to my management team. I know what I want, and we're on our way to getting it."

"This all sounds like it turned out the way it was supposed to," Hugh said with a satisfied smile.

"Well . . . ," responded Max, "it hasn't actually turned out *yet*, but I've already seen some signs of things changing. For example, the leaders in one local corporation have changed how they view minority/majority joint venture relationships. Being certified is now just the beginning for the minority business. The corporation is asking the potential partners to have a specific plan for the joint venture to move increasingly toward sustainability. They want to see these partnerships provide more value than simply adding to the minority spending total. They're using the questions we recommended as a framework for their review."

"That could negatively affect the organization's level of minority spending if they stop counting some of those relationships," Fenton remarked.

"Maybe in the short run," Max responded. "But long term, people will understand what sustainable models look like, and they'll respond to the higher expectations. The company leaders decided they wanted their diverse spending to be more meaningful. One of the hospital systems went as far as creating an ad hoc committee to review joint ventures on the basis of their sustainability. Trust me, that will change behavior."

"Wow. They're serious about fixing joint ventures. Is evaluating them like this even legal?" Fenton asked.

"No one has found it a question of legality. Corporations can decide to do business with whomever they want, generally for the reasons they decide. I've even had calls from government agencies trying to determine how they might write the joint venture sustainability criteria into policy. I'm sure that'll create legal questions, but we'll see," Max explained.

"This additional focus on joint ventures isn't the only action our local major organizations have taken. Many of the CEOs decided they wanted more transparency in their reporting of diverse spending. Others are working hard to drive the responsibility and accountability for diverse spending out into the business units, not just have it be the job of the supplier diversity department. And of course, leaders in some organizations thought that what they've been doing is good enough. It meets what they regard as the industry standards for supplier diversity, and they see no need to change. One CEO told me privately he was going to slowly shut down the company's supplier diversity effort. He never believed in the business case, and he'd heard nothing over the years to change his mind."

"Mixed results for sure," Hugh agreed. "But it's clear. Changing their habits is the first step to changing their outcomes."

"Changing my personal habits was *my* first step, that's for sure," Fenton offered. "I needed to broaden my view of business and entrepreneurship. So I'm now reading *The Wall Street Journal* every day and I joined the Deal Makers Club. This group meets for lunch and features a speaker once a month. So I get to hear about successful business models and at the same time meet other entrepreneurs, bankers, and investors. It's still new, but it's already impacting my thinking and our business activity."

"Really? In what ways?" Max asked, turning to look at Fenton.

"First, we realized it was dangerous for our business to stay where it was. We needed a strategy to become more valuable to our customers. And that meant pushing ourselves toward global competitiveness. So we've taken small steps. We're in talks about merging one of our divisions with the business of one of the members of my CEO Roundtable. He was being forced to close his company, but he had access to some great customers. The merger would immediately diversify our customer base and over the next twelve months, it would improve our financial position. The bank will like that," Fenton said smiling. "Access to more capital will allow us to continue to pursue potential acquisitions in the northwest region of the country. This will build our national presence and also position us to access the important Asian market over the next few years. We've been active, but that's what it takes."

"You've learned a lot through this process," Hugh said, looking impressed.

"Hugh, honestly it's not what I learned that mattered the most; it's what I came to *understand*. I now understand the power in the question *What would I do if I weren't a minority-owned business?* That question released me to be the best entrepreneur I can be based on *all* of the factors, my race being just one of them!" Fenton explained, obviously energized.

"Gentlemen, you two are something," said Hugh, slowly making his way to his feet. "You know I rely on you guys to keep me young. So thanks for taking me along for the ride." With a wave of his hand, he started shuffling down the pathway. He stopped, turned and looked back as the two men watched him walk away.

"And you make a pretty good team, too!" Hugh called out. "You never know. Maybe you can do something together one day."

The two men looked at each other and smiled.

"Does Hugh know something we don't know?" Fenton asked. "My experience with him suggest he probably does," Max replied with a confident smile.

What to Do Next

Now that you've seen the minority business development environment through a number of perspectives, what do you do? The short answer is this: Do *something*!

I suggest pulling the "big ideas" from this fable and candidly review your own situation by asking:

- What have you come to understand from reading *What Is the Color of Opportunity?*
- Which of the lessons are likely to have the greatest impact on you and your organization?
- Which are you committed to act on right away? Consider the ideas that matter most to your ability to reach your goals and objectives. Start with those.
- How can you make these ideas a part of how you do business?
- Visit our website at www.ColorofOpportunity.com for additional information and support.

Remember, *there is no color of opportunity.* Yes, there are always things we can understand better and specific actions that lead to better outcomes. But nothing changes until we change our attitudes, broaden our perspectives, and enhance our expectations. You'll find new realities at the crossroads of business and race—and that's also where you'll discover your opportunities for success.

It is the difference between interest and commitment.

APPENDIX A

RECOMMENDATIONS FOR COMMITTED MAJOR BUYING ORGANIZATIONS

These recommendations were created to provide specific guidance to major buying organizations who desire to make their spending with minority owned firms more meaningful. These actions generally cost little to nothing to implement but have the capability to drive your organization to new levels of achievement and impact.

There are many ways you can apply these recommendations. Here are three quick ideas to get you started:

1. Compare these recommendations to your current approach.

2. Use the recommendations in discussions with peers both internal and external to your company. Collectively look for ways to implement the ideas.

3. Consult the recommendations as you do your annual planning or as you create new strategies for supplier diversity.

Recommendations for Committed Major Buying Organizations

Be resolved. And show it. The biggest difference between interest and commitment is the level of resolve. Commitment doesn't cost more, but it does demand more. Being resolved means using the same level of effort and resources you would for other initiatives that matter to your organization.

- **Approach supplier diversity like you would other areas of business.** Do with supplier diversity what you've done with initiatives like safety, quality, and cost reduction. Use a combination of talent, objectives, resources, success metrics, and accountability.

- **Don't accept the either/or argument**. The argument of either/or says "you can *either* get increased minority spending *or* you can get lower cost, higher quality, better delivery, broader reach, or whatever else you want in product and service delivery." An either/or argument implies you can't have both. This argument—really an excuse—is also the reason still used to explain why doing business with minorities is difficult and goes against an organization's best interest. Refuse to accept the either/or argument and *demand* both. Yes, this might be difficult but so was space travel, getting the voters rights act passed, and desegregating schools.

- **Spread accountability.** Most organizations *push* supplier diversity onto the other parts of their businesses. Doing that often results in a built-in tension or resistance to the supplier diversity effort. It puts the leader of supplier diversity into a position of *chasing down* the individuals who buy things and trying to *push* them into considering a diverse supplier. A more effective dynamic happens when various segments of the business *pull* supplier diversity through the organization. Diversifying your base of suppliers will remain difficult until the accountability for doing so is shared across the organization. To do that, set performance targets, add supplier diversity to evaluation criteria, and build in incentives like internal awards and recognition.

Be candid. One of the complexities of dealing with race issues is a fear of providing candid feedback. Yet candor is critical in building a diverse base of competitive suppliers. Using candor isn't only for the suppliers; it's also for internal personnel struggling to embrace this initiative.

- **Acknowledge internal hurdles**. Doing business with major organizations is not easy; their size and complexity can be difficult to navigate. In addition, the level of your organization's commitment to doing business with minority firms likely differs from department to department and person to person. Acknowledge this reality in your internal and external communications. Focus your attention on internal metrics, reporting, and education to increase consistency in your approach to diverse suppliers.

- **Explain the criteria for success.** Be sure to tell potential minority suppliers where they fall short. Successful suppliers of tomorrow need to hear your clear, specific, and candid feedback. Suppliers will rise to the expectations of the customer, so make sure they understand what those expectations are.

- **Encourage potential.** But don't lead supplier firms on. Some suppliers are not ready to work with your organization while others, for many reasons, will likely never succeed in your environment. Know the difference and make it clear where they stand and why. It doesn't mean their businesses are not good; it simply means they're not a fit for your organization. Your candor will allow them to pursue opportunities with other organizations. Remember, it's costly for a potential supplier to pursue your business especially when they have a low probability of winning.

Be bold. Major buying organizations have been too conservative in their expectations for results from their minority business efforts. Most of them are in a unique position to influence outcomes because they have the leverage only a major customer can have. The opportunity is to use their leverage to set up an environment of high expectations. Some would call it bold, but it's actually consistent with the actions businesses take with other initiatives.

- **Avoid the spending goal *coup.*** Don't let the spending goal take over the true meaning. Ask yourself if this arrangement would make sense if you weren't trying to reach a spending goal? If the answer is "no" then it probably isn't meaningful. Yes, *how much* you spend is important, but it's not as important as *how* you spend your dollars. Be willing to spend less as you make your spending more meaningful.

- **Make inclusion a criterion for suppliers.** Finding a diverse solution must be one of the performance criterion for your suppliers—not a "nice to have" but a "must deliver." Asking, requesting, and suggesting is *not* enough. Suppliers must respond to customer needs. So make a willingness to do business with diverse suppliers a need and measure their performance in meeting that need.

- **Question minority/major relationships.** Your spending is meaningful when it contributes to the growth of sustainable diverse suppliers. Be particularly careful doing business with minority/majority joint ventures and strategic alliances. Many are a new spin on an old practice that primarily benefits the majority business. Answer the litmus test questions in Appendix B to assist your evaluation.

- **Increase your expectations for minority suppliers.**
  Limit communicating with the firms that are only interested in getting a contract. Reward the firms who take a
  strategic view on pricing, product mix, and the selection
  of partners. They get the contract because they can support your needs and become truly successful when they
  develop their capacity to succeed. Invest only in the firms
  worthy of your investment. Invest with your time, your
  support, and your money when the opportunity is right.

APPENDIX B

LITMUS TEST QUESTIONS FOR MINORITY/MAJORITY RELATIONSHIPS

Evaluating formal relationships between minority and majority organizations has never been an exact science but answering the questions below can assist in that assessment. If your answers are "no" or "doubtful," then the relationship offers a limited opportunity to create a sustainable minority enterprise.

These questions can be used by major buying organizations as a means of evaluating the authenticity of a minority/majority relationship you may be considering doing business with.

This guide is also helpful to both minority and majority companies looking to build a business model that is sustainable.

Litmus Test Questions for Minority/Majority Relationships

1. Is the minority partner building a competitive market positioning separate from its majority joint venture partner?

2. Is the minority entity growing any specific, tangible, measurable, independent capability (e.g., new processes, additional management talent, increasing portion of the flow of dollars from contracts)?

3. Does the relationship deliver any value beyond increased minority spending?

4. Is the minority participant building equity?

5. Is the joint venture creating a valued enterprise the minority partner can one day sell?

ABOUT THE AUTHOR

D r. Melvin Gravely II is the founder of the Institute for Entrepreneurial Thinking, Ltd. a think tank with a mission to improve the results of minority business development activities. He is an advisor to communities, business support organizations, major corporations, and minority businesses across the nation.

A popular speaker and noted thought leader in minority business development, Dr. Gravely is the editor of *The Diverse Business Dialogue* and *The Entrepreneurial Thinker* newsletters. He has written six books, including three others in this series: *When Black and White Make Green, The Lost Art of Entrepreneurship*, and *Getting to the Next Level*.

Dr. Gravely has a BS in computer science from Mount Union College and an MBA from Kent State University. He earned his doctorate in business administration and entrepreneurship from the Union Institute and University. He currently lives in Cincinnati with his family.

OTHER BOOKS IN THE SERIES BY MEL GRAVELY

I f you enjoyed this book, you will also like reading the previous three books in the series. In *The Lost Art of Entrepreneurship*, *When Black and White Make Green* and *Getting to The Next Level,* you will encounter many of the characters you enjoyed in this book, including wise old Hugh, Fenton, Carol, and Max. The other three books are all powerful stories full of practical lessons and solid strategies. The reads are quick and entertaining, and the proven approaches create lasting results.

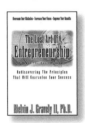

The Lost Art of Entrepreneurship
Rediscovering the Principles That Will
Guarantee Your Success

When Black and White Make Green
The Next Evolution in Business & Race

Getting to the Next Level
Business, Race and Our Common Goal
to Be Competitive

YOUR FEEDBACK PLEASE

We want to hear from you. What did you think of *What Is the Color of Opportunity*? How did the book affect your business, supplier program, or community efforts? Tell us about your success stories discussing and implementing the ideas.

You can email us at: info@entrethinking.com

or

Institute for Entrepreneurial Thinking, Ltd.
Attn: What Is the Color of Opportunity?
P.O. Box 621170
Cincinnati, OH 45262-1170

You can find the tools referenced in
What Is the Color of Opportunity?
and more at
www.ColorofOpportunity.com